FLOATING THROUGH
FRANCE

FLOATING THROUGH
FRANCE

Cruising the inland waterways to the Med

Kerry and Fraser Buchanan

ADLARD
COLES

LONDON · OXFORD · NEW YORK · NEW DELHI · SYDNEY

ADLARD COLES
Bloomsbury Publishing Plc
50 Bedford Square, London, WC1B 3DP, UK
Bloomsbury Publishing Ireland Limited,
29 Earlsfort Terrace, Dublin 2, D02 AY28, Ireland

BLOOMSBURY, ADLARD COLES and the Adlard Coles logo are trademarks of
Bloomsbury Publishing Plc

First published in Great Britain 2026

A catalogue record for this book is available from the British Library

Library of Congress Cataloguing-in-Publication data has been applied for

ISBN: PB: 978-1-3994-2735-7; ePDF: 978-1-3994-2734-0; ePub: 978-1-3994-2733-3

2 4 6 8 10 9 7 5 3 1

Typeset in Bulmer by Phil Beresford

Printed and bound in China by Toppan Leefung Printing

To find out more about our authors and books visit www.bloomsbury.com and sign up for our newsletters
For product safety related questions contact productsafety@bloomsbury.com

Dedication

To the Royal National Lifeboat Institute: unpaid volunteers who put their lives on the line to help others day and night, 365 days a year. Thank you for your generosity of spirit and your bravery.

CONTENTS

PART 3: An Honorary Barge

PART 4: Remembering how to sail

Appendices

⬆ *Fraser and Kerry*

INTRODUCTION

Meet the crew

Alove of the sea runs in the blood in some families. When Fraser and I met at university, neither of us had much sailing experience, but our mutual love of water had shown itself in other ways. Fraser was a competitive swimmer; I had rowed for my university. Sailing together was a natural progression and not long after we married, we discovered flotilla holidays where pretty much anyone could have a go (in those days they didn't ask for any qualifications).

With two decent incomes and no kids, we splashed out on a couple of weeks in Greece and somehow managed not to run aground or crash into anything or anyone. That was when the addiction really took hold.

As the years passed, Fraser built a small plywood dinghy which we sailed until my first pregnancy bump prevented me ducking under the boom. After that it was a Skipper 17 trailer sailor with First Baby engulfed by the smallest baby lifejacket available and clipped in, still inside her rocking car seat. As two more bumps appeared and developed into sprogs we needed more space, so we bought a 26ft Westerly Centaur, still one of my favourite boats.

We sailed with the children on Lough Neagh, a huge freshwater lake in Northern Ireland, and they learned to swim in its murky waters. I told them that if they put their feet down, they'd stand on eels, so they quickly became competent and fast swimmers. They grew up eating from tins of hot dog sausages warmed on rocks at the edge of the red embers of a campfire on Ram's Island. They learned to tie knots, make shelters and track animals like proper little wildlings.

As they outgrew the Centaur's berths, we were forced to scale up to a Southerly 105, which, when Lough Neagh became too small for us, we took down the River Bann to the sea near Coleraine. That was when our interest in canals and locks began, as we spotted kingfishers and otters along the riverbank.

I should point out that we were always sailing on a very tight budget. We could only afford old boats, and Fraser carried out all the maintenance, which mostly consisted of repairing anything that broke. Perhaps it shouldn't have come as a surprise when we lost our steering one bright June day while sailing a brisk close-reach roughly opposite the Giant's Causeway.

Although we could have got back on our own with the emergency tiller and autopilot, the RNLI, hearing that we had children on board, sent out the Portrush Lifeboat which towed us to safety. The wind was onshore, and the sea conditions were described by the laconic Coxswain of the lifeboat as 'a bit choppy'. There are few sights more welcome than that splash of blue and orange with a creaming white bow wave as it powers through the waves towards you. Those fellas are the best.

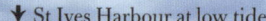
⤓ St Ives Harbour at low tide

I'm not sure if it was the lifeboat rescue that put Middle Child off sailing or the time we almost sank (leaking stern gland). Or maybe it was the constant seasickness.

Around that time, I was diagnosed with psoriatic arthritis which meant giving up my career as a vet. One rheumatology consultant had forecast that I'd be in a wheelchair by the time I was 50, a frightening thought, but luckily, he'd overstated the case. However, painful joints and the lack of balance that comes with them did alter our lives significantly. I wasn't sure if I'd ever sail again.

With the children losing interest in sailing, we sold the Southerly, so they could pursue nice, safe, land-based activities such as horse riding, whitewater kayaking and mountain biking.

A decade or so later, after various arthritis treatments, most of which have yucky side effects that include severe nausea and a slowly dying liver, we decided that I wasn't deteriorating too fast and we were prepared to give it a go again. Surely the French canals were just the place to take a disease that improves with sunlight?

The children were all grown up by then, and almost independent by the time Fraser and I managed to scrape together the money to buy another boat. We'd been talking for a couple of decades about taking our own boat through the French canals, and had hoped to do it with the Southerly, the perfect boat with her swing keel and low draught, but the timing had never been quite right.

In 2018 we set off boat shopping again, with shallow draught as one of our main criteria. Eventually, after several false starts, we discovered *Barberry*, a 1984 Barbican 33 with a long keel.

Flash forward to summer 2020. In the midst of Covid lockdown Fraser received a diagnosis of prostate cancer, my dad was in the final stages of dementia, we had a farm with a menagerie of horses, dogs and cats that needed us, and my mobility was decreasing. We both felt as though a clock was ticking. We longed to escape though we couldn't see how it would be possible.

You should be careful what you wish for. The year 2022 turned out to be a double-edged sword. My dad finally succumbed to his illness, our one remaining elderly horse keeled over in the field and died, and we lost both our wonderful dogs, one to old age, the second, devastatingly, to stomach cancer.

However, to balance the horror, Fraser finally received the all clear from his cancer specialist, although the 'shot across the bows' pushed him into taking early retirement; Covid had become a horror story in the rear-view mirror; we sold the farm, and suddenly we were free. We moved into a rented house ten minutes away from the marina and really stepped up the preparations for our departure. In his retirement speech, Fraser described our adventure as sailing south until he could jump into the sea without screaming.

We still had two cats living with us (one elderly, the other disabled), but Middle Child (the seasick one) was beginning to write up her PhD thesis so we bribed her with free accommodation in return for house- and cat-sitting for up to 6 months.

Finally, the stars seemed aligned for an early spring 2023 departure.

⚓ Barberry *under a lifting bridge*

PART 1

Festina Lente

Corsica

Italy

Greece

Sardinia   Sicily

1

CHOOSING A BOAT

Our prospective voyage had three main elements, each of which required its own specific preparation and particular boat characteristics.

Phase 1

Cold, tidal waters of UK and northern France, with strong winds, rain, fog, etc.

The boat has to be seaworthy, warm, watertight, and able to cope with the unexpected in terms of sea state. Good navigation equipment is required for busy shipping lanes. A watertight ship's bucket for… Never mind. You'll read about it later.

Phase 2

French rivers and canals with no sailing (or mast, for that matter), going from cool to hot and sunny as we headed south.

We needed limited draught, as the canals can be shallow, depending on the season and the weather. We also needed protection and manoeuvrability for passing through locks, some way to communicate with lock keepers when our mast (and therefore radio aerial) was down, and protection from the elements, especially the sun as we moved further south. Also, we knew we would have strictly limited air draught beneath many of the bridges and in the tunnels. Perhaps most important was a reliable engine, and a way to clear weed from the cooling water intake.

Phase 3

The Mediterranean. France, Corsica (both French speaking); Sardinia, Sicily, Italy (all Italian speaking) and finally Greece.

Depth would no longer be an issue in the Med, but sailing capability in both strong winds and light airs would be beneficial. Protection from the sun would be essential for this phase, as well as a reliable anchoring system.

We would be meeting the challenges of Med Mooring for the first time, which involves being able to go stern-to in tight spaces. We also needed a reliable dinghy and a way to store it other than towing it all the time.

We had several essential criteria when we set about searching for a boat. Initially, we gave ourselves a budget of around £10,000 and had a boat length of 26–30ft

(8–9m) in mind – until we began viewing boats and realised that we'd both become less bendy with age, and that to achieve standing headroom for two tallish people, we'd need to go a bit longer.

Other criteria included shoal draught, a sea-kindly boat able to withstand the ferocious weather around Ireland and Scotland yet suitable for shorthanded sailing, a reliable engine, good rigging and sails and a comfortable cabin for long-term living aboard.

Our budget quickly stretched, and we discovered that most of the promising boats were in the

Key:
— Sea routes
— Tidal Seine
— Canals and non-tidal rivers
— Saône and Rhône rivers

⬆ *Summary of the route from Northern Ireland to Greece*

⚓ Barberry *the day we bought her*

south of England so we drew up a shortlist, then flew over there to hunt for the perfect boat.

Sadly, the one on which we placed a deposit (subject to survey), having viewed her only in the water, received the worst survey report we'd ever seen. The surveyor phoned us partway through and asked if we wanted him to continue. Everything below the waterline spelled trouble, and in addition her decks were soggy. To be fair to Fraser, I think he had been dazzled by her shiny new engine which blinded him to all her faults!

Downhearted, we went back to the drawing board, having spent a significant chunk of our budget on travel hoists, surveys and flights to Southampton. Then we saw

Barberry advertised, just a couple of hours' drive from us. As soon as I saw her photograph in the advert, I fell for her lines.

Barberry is a 1984 Maurice Griffiths-designed Barbican 33 with a long keel and centreplate. With the plate up, she draws around 4ft (1.2m) (the maximum published depth for the routes we hoped to take is 6ft/1.8m), yet she's strong, stable, and sails extremely comfortably (if not very swiftly, at least with us in charge), a go-anywhere cruiser that still boasts shoal draught.

She'd been immaculately kept by her owners, but as they'd retired from boat to camper van, she'd been out of the water for a few years until they gradually accepted that

⚓ Barberry *being launched for the first time after purchase*

their sailing days were over.

A survey showed her to be in exceptional condition and a deal was struck. We sailed her back from Coleraine to her new home in Bangor (County Down, not the Welsh one) and she behaved perfectly.

For a boat knocking on the door of 35 years old, she was pristine. When she was launched after we bought her, one of the helpers scrambled aboard to check the bilges. He was gone far too long, and Fraser and I were beginning to sweat. Finally, he popped his head up through the companionway, holding one finger aloft. Had he found water in the bilges?

'A speck of dust,' he cried. 'Took me a while, but I found one.'

Everything on the boat was dated, but even when you buy a younger boat there'll always be some upgrades necessary. You'd think that after so many years of boat ownership we'd have lost some of our naivety, but apparently not. It took us five years to prepare her for the voyage we had planned, and we spent much more again than the original purchase price.

We each made a list of essential upgrades. Fraser's was quite short; mine ran to several pages. *See Appendix 1 for upgrading cost summary.*

Anyone else thinking of doing something similar will have their own priorities, probably very different from ours, but that's what makes boating so interesting: the infinite variety of boats and the lucky people who sail them. At the very least, they can read our idea of necessary upgrades, then snort in a superior manner as they add an ice maker or washing machine to their own list of essentials.

Lessons Learned

- Boat choice is always a compromise. We would have liked a little more internal space, better windward performance and a boat that steers going astern.

- Always get a boat surveyed.

- No boat excels at every challenge (although *Barberry* comes pretty close).

- Everyone has a different notion of the ideal boat and which upgrades are important.

2

FITTING OUT THE BOAT

First we fitted a new chart plotter, because our ageing eyesight struggled with the tiny one that came with *Barberry*, and that was the beginning of a landslide of new additions. It's a bit like painting one wall in your lounge because the dog has trailed muddy fur all along it and it won't scrub clean. Suddenly, all the other walls look grubby in comparison, so you end up redecorating the entire house. Or maybe that's just me.

We ended up with AIS (Automatic Identification System), new autopilot, new radar, bigger solar panels to help run all the gizmos, an additional battery, a better battery charger, etc.

The three most expensive upgrades we made were the engine, a bow thruster and new upholstery. A luxury, you might think, but in warmer climates, the original vinyl seats and mattresses would have been sweaty and uncomfortable. Besides, the foam was well flattened by 35 years of use.

The engine represented peace of mind, plus it was quieter and more economical than the original Thorneycroft, which was beginning to show a reluctance to start in cold weather that rivalled my reluctance to surface from a warm duvet between November and May. For navigating the French inland waterways, a reliable engine is a huge comfort.

The bow thruster was a harder decision as they're often ridiculed by 'proper sailors', but we'd tried very hard to learn to go astern in *Barberry* without one, even taking advice from two different RYA instructors. One caused a nasty scratch in the gel coat, the other said boats like *Barberry* are what bow thrusters are designed for. It

➤ *Fraser fitting keel cooler for fridge*

FITTING OUT THE BOAT

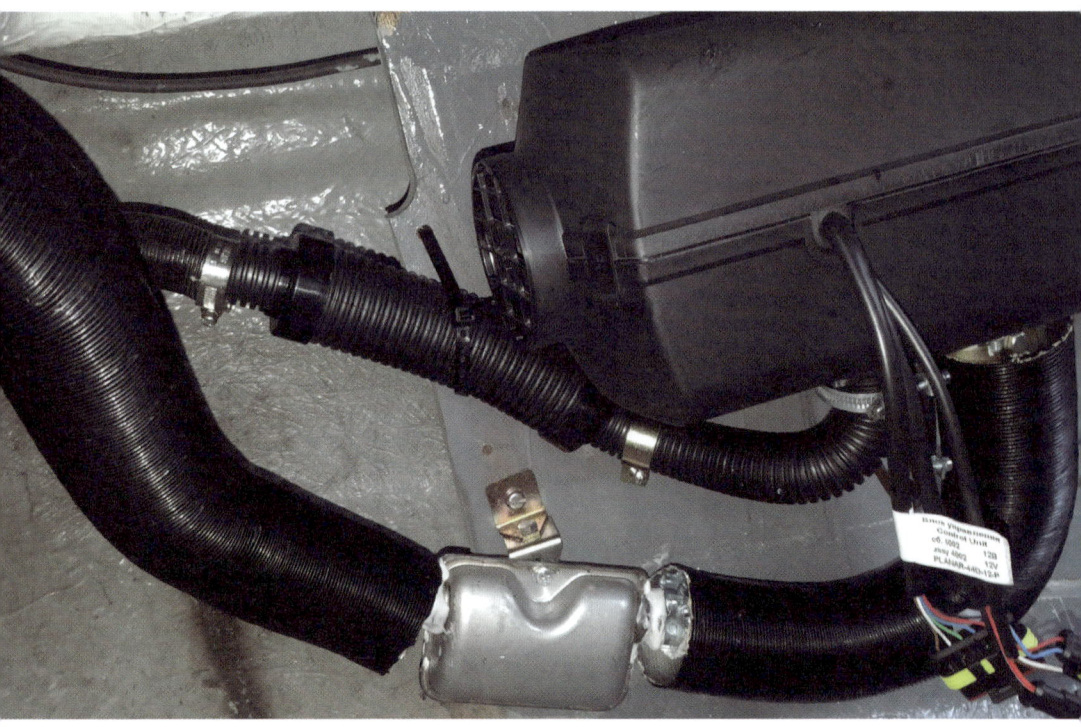

↟ *Autoterm cabin heater*

began to earn its keep in the French canals but really came into its own when we started having to Med Moor. (See Part 4: Remembering how to sail)

Barberry came with an original cavernous cool box. Fraser added thick insulation around the outside, then a keel-cooled refrigeration system to increase efficiency in warmer climes and keep power demand to a minimum. A new seal for the cool box lid completed the conversion and it has worked a treat ever since.

After the fridge came a cabin heater to replace the non-functioning museum piece that came with the boat. Although we knew we'd be unlikely to need it once we reached the Med, there were some cold miles to sail before we got that far, and we were grateful for it. Besides, maybe we'll spend some winters in the Med!

Typically, the new piping was wider in diameter than the existing ductwork, which led to Fraser playing a solo game of Twister as he contorted his upper body into tiny cupboards and lockers, drilling slightly wider holes six times through various bulkheads. Sometimes the drill would snag, and his arm would rotate, rather than the drill, but that's boat jobs for you. I assisted him with useful comments like, 'Ooh, the next one looks even harder,' and, 'I can't wait until you're finished. It's freezing in here.'

We also decided we needed to increase our freshwater storage. *Barberry* came with a 200-litre

⚓ *Holding tank*

↑ *One of the new water tanks*

a fancy tap. Now we no longer need to carry bottled water on the boat (except a couple for emergencies and some smaller ones in our grab bag), our water tastes wonderful, and we know it's safe.

Another essential before we set off was a holding tank. For a 33ft old-school yacht (narrower in the beam than most modern production yachts), *Barberry* possesses a surprising number of useful nooks and crannies. Fraser managed to fit a 63-litre holding tank beneath the sink in the heads, and while he was at it, he replaced the Blakes toilet pump with a new one, keeping the original for spares. He also added rather ugly anti-syphon loops above the waterline, but safety comes before aesthetics.

Nothing ever seems to go wrong with the Blakes Lavac toilet. We've had other brands in previous boats, and they might look prettier, but I know which I prefer. The only slight shortcoming is the vacuumed-down toilet seat after flushing. We usually ask each other, 'Anyone else need to go or will I flush?'

Occasionally one of us forgets to do this, and then the next user must cross their legs or clench their butt cheeks until it unsticks again, which seems to take forever. Still,

flexible tank sited beneath the forward berth, but much of that space was now taken up by the bow thruster tunnel.

Fraser squeezed in two 70-litre rigid tanks, one each side beneath the V-berth. He also replaced the flexible tank with a new 100-litre one, giving us 240 litres of fresh water on board, plus another 40 litres that we carried in canisters on deck.

Despite replacing tanks and all the piping, our drinking water still tasted of boat, so after much research, we ordered a UV water steriliser that came with a filter and the vacuum does release eventually, and no one has admitted to damp underwear (or worse) so far.

Another upgrade that I pretty much demanded was a bigger dinghy than the little Avon that came with *Barberry*. From the perspective of an overweight woman with dodgy joints and poor balance, descending the ladder into it equated to diving from one of those platforms hundreds

⚓ *UV steriliser*

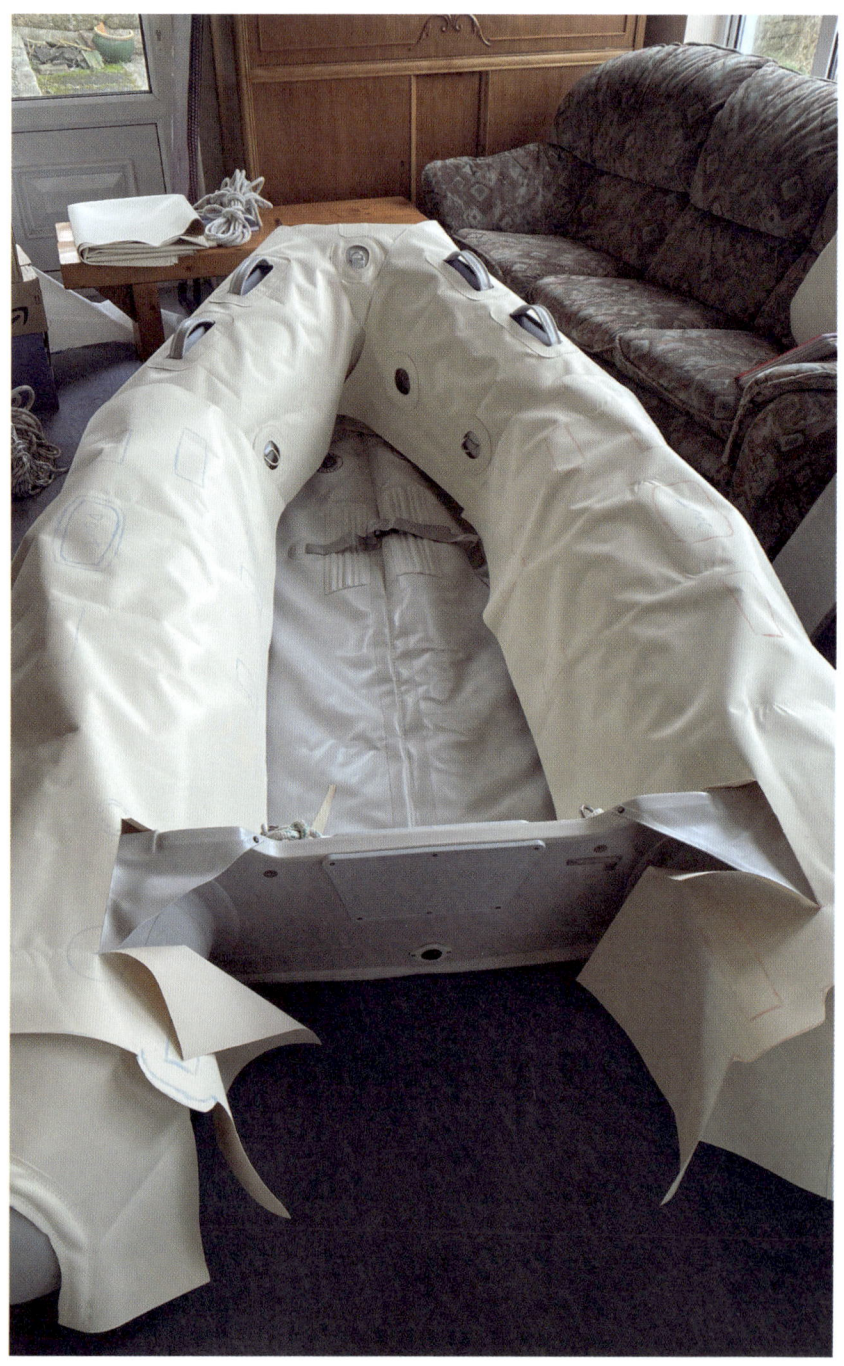

⬆ *Chaps in progress*

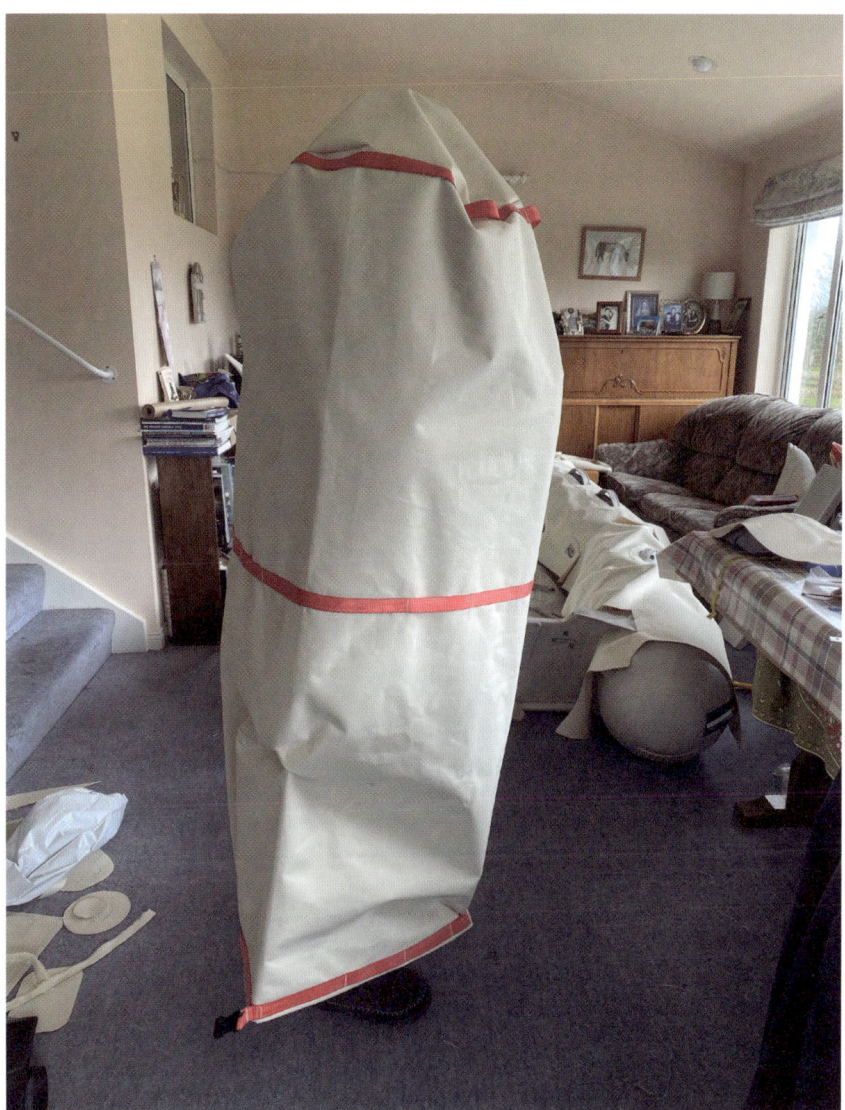

⬆ *Kerry modelling the dinghy bag*

of feet high and landing in a tiny swimming pool for the amusement of an audience that is only there to see the diver miss.

Fraser fitted davits to *Barberry's* aft coaming, then we bought a 2.7m Honwave dinghy with a load capacity that even I was happy with. We'd seen dinghy chaps on several YouTube sailing channels based in the Med, designed to protect the PVC tubes from UV rays, but they seemed impossible to find locally,

⬆ Top: *Upholstery before*; above: *Upholstery after*

so Fraser bought some canvas on eBay, absconded with my sewing machine, and set to work.

Fraser was off work for a long period while he received radiotherapy for his prostate cancer, so he had time on his hands. I think the enormous challenge of fitting these complicated chaps helped take his mind off the medical stuff.

That dinghy remained inflated in our dining room for months (all the furniture pushed to one end, out of the way) while Fraser draped strips of canvas over the tubes and drew on it with tailor's chalk. After it was finished, he made hatch covers, winch covers, and a matching bag for storing the rolled-up dinghy. If I'd stood still long enough, he'd probably have made a cover for me.

With some long and challenging passages ahead of us, we put safety high on our list of priorities, so a new life raft, fire extinguishers (including an automatic one for the engine bay), automatic bilge pump, new masthead lights and VHF aerial were all installed. We attached personal AIS man overboard beacons to each of our lifejackets, and an EPIRB (Emergency Position Indicating Radio Beacon) for the boat.

As we hoped to remain independent and as close to off-grid as possible, we replaced our solar panels with bigger, more efficient ones, including a 100W flexible panel, giving us a total of 200W of solar. It doesn't sound like much, but we don't carry many electrical luxuries on board.

We tried to order a bespoke bimini, but the local suppliers all shrugged and shook their heads. It wasn't a straightforward job, as *Barberry*'s mainsheet comes down into the centre of her cockpit, in front of the steering position. On our travels we noticed that small boats rarely have effective biminis. We set off without and accepted that we'd probably fry despite the parasol we used for shade (spoiler: we did fry). It was the following year, with *Barberry* based in Greece, before Fraser managed to design and make a bimini and cockpit cover that do the job perfectly.

On the whole, we've done things as economically as possible and many of the jobs were carried out by Fraser, with much muffled grunting and some sticky epoxy fingerprints on the varnished woodwork to prove it. For more specialist jobs, such as fitting the bow-thruster and most of the electronics, we used professionals. Similarly the new engine, standing rigging and upholstery were fitted by local companies. This was money well spent, and many of these people have become good friends and have provided advice long distance.

For the bow thruster and most of the electronics we called in our local Raymarine specialist, Brian, who cheerfully took on all the jobs we asked of him and kept us entertained with his dry, sarcastic humour. He's become a good friend over the years and even gives long distance advice by phone when something stops working. 'Turn it off and then back on', usually.

The engine was professionally fitted by Michael of Coburn Marine Engineering, who managed to complete the work and conduct sea trials with the first Covid lockdown breathing down his neck, and we used a professional rigger to replace the standing rigging. We also used a professional marine upholstery company to make our new seating cushions and bed mattresses. That was money well spent.

There were many more upgrades, and if you really want to see the detail, a full list is in Appendix 1.

Lessons Learned

- Even a well-cared-for boat will need work and money spent on it.

- Electronics go out of date quickly.

- Sometimes luxuries are worth the extra money.

- Many boat jobs can be carried out by a determined amateur, but some are better undertaken by professionals.

3

FITTING OUT OURSELVES

When we bought *Barberry* in 2018, it had been nearly ten years since we'd sailed regularly and in those days we'd had a teenaged crew to do all the exciting bits, like jumping with lines when we were too far from the quay (and usually moving away).

We were both older, less able, had lost our confidence and had forgotten how to navigate. There was a steep learning curve ahead of us. However, we were no longer full-time taxi drivers for a bunch of ungrateful teenagers, and some of our income was left at the end of each month, which was a novel experience.

The list of paperwork we needed for our voyage seemed scarily long.

For us:
- Radio operator's licence
- ICC (International Certificate of Competence)
- CEVNI (European Code for Inland Waterways)
- Irish passports (*see Appendices 3 & 4*)
- British passports (*see Appendix 3*).

For the boat:
- Ship's Radio Licence
- Small Ships registration (SSR)
- Original Bill of Sale showing VAT paid
- Proof of location for Brexit date (31st December 2020)
- Vignette (a pass that allows you free access to the entire inland waterway system of France and free mooring on the banks when possible).

When Covid hit, and we were locked down on the farm with our menagerie of family and animals, we decided it was time to gather the qualifications we'd been too busy to work for in all our years of sailing. We both did an online course to gain our Day Skipper Theory (we weren't competitive at all), followed by our Yachtmaster Coastal Theory.

We were mutually supportive when one of us didn't quite get the calculations correct the first time as we relearned old skills, but when it came to the exams, we fought for every single percentage point. Fortunately, we ended up with almost identical scores each time, which might possibly have saved our marriage.

After this, we needed to achieve at least the Day Skipper practical, which we arranged through a lovely man who kept his boat near *Barberry* in Bangor Marina. Rusty McGovern is a sailor of the storybook type – his wild hair and beard, the creases from staring into wind and sun, and the twinkle in his eyes. He's also an RYA examiner and runs Sailschool NI.

We were both ridiculously nervous on the big day, but he soon put us at our ease.

'I've seen you guys out there in all weathers, and I've seen you manoeuvring at close quarters in the marina. You have absolutely nothing to worry about.'

That vote of confidence gave us both such a lift, as I'm sure he knew it would, and we each managed to demonstrate all the required skills, taking turns at catching mooring buoys, berthing the boat (forwards and backwards, just for the fun of it) and all the rest of the challenges that had been keeping us both awake for weeks.

With our Day Skippers signed off, we were able to apply for an ICC (International Certificate of Competence) through the RYA (Royal Yachting Association), which made us legal to sail in the EU. We also studied for and gained the CEVNI (Code Européen des Voies de Navigation Intérieure) qualification for the inland waterways section (then promptly forgot all the signs and signals again, until we had to use them in earnest).

Since Brexit, holders of British passports only have a rolling 90 days in 180 in which they are allowed to stay within the Schengen Zone, which includes all the countries we needed to pass through as well as Greece, where we hoped to be based for a long time. We estimated that it would take us between four and six months to reach Greece: far more than our allotted 90 days. *See Appendices 3 & 4.*

The best solution for us was to apply for Irish passports. There are several ways this can be done, but the only one open to us was by becoming Irish citizens through our grandparents. Each of us had a grandmother born in Ireland (mine was from County Mayo, and Fraser's was from County Down, Northern Ireland, but she lived pre-partition, so that still counted as Irish). We applied just as Covid hit, so our applications became lost in the backlogged system, and it was two years, and a lot of money, before those treasured burgundy folders arrived in the post. Now we had freedom of movement within the Schengen Zone (with the added bonus of avoiding the non-EU queues in airports!).

Interestingly, we were only asked for our paperwork once between home and Greece, and even then the French VNF official only wanted to see our vignette for the inland waterways, but when we reached Greece, we needed EVERYTHING!

Between buying *Barberry* in 2018 and setting off on our adventure in 2023, we tried to build miles in as many conditions as we could. We sailed down the east coast of Ireland as far south as Greystones as well as to Scotland. We became gradually more confident, and grew to know *Barberry* well, when to reef, how to set a safe gybe preventer, when to start the engine, and when to turn back. All valuable lessons.

By winter of 2022/23, almost all the boat jobs were complete. We lifted her out one last time in Bangor and Fraser changed all her original bronze through-hulls and seacocks for composite ones. As it turns out they were solid bronze and they'd probably have been good for another 40 years, but the only way to find that out for sure was to remove them, and that's a destructive process.

Lessons Learned

- We're not as young as we used to be.

- Old dogs can still learn new tricks (or relearn old ones).

- We're more competent than we thought we were.

- Never diss your Irish grandma: she can come in useful, even when she's long gone.

Overleaf: Fraser helming, east coast of Ireland

4

PASSAGE PLANNING

Greece felt a very long way from the north of Ireland, but planning the routes we'd take was one of the things that kept me sane through the difficult years when I was caring for my father, who had dementia.

Immersing myself in pilot books (*See Appendix 5*) and making copious notes on passage times, marina and harbour details, anchorages, locks and lifting bridges was a way to dream of sunshine during dark times, although, at that stage, we had no idea *when* or even *if* we would ever be able to set off on our adventure.

Fraser would come in, tired from work after a long commute, and raise an eyebrow. 'You do know we're not going for a while, don't you?' He found it hard to dream when we had no actual escape plan.

But when it came to spring 2023, all my research paid off. I'd formed some useful contacts via the Facebook group *Women on Barges*, and others, and was able to say with confidence that after the 2022 drought conditions in France, followed by a drier than usual winter, we would need to hit the French canals as early in the season as possible if we wanted to make it through before they started closing reaches due to lack of water.

Lessons Learned

- No matter how much planning you do in advance, the sea and the weather will throw unexpected challenges at you.

- It's still worth being as thoroughly prepared as possible. My detailed research paid off in many ways.

- Be aware of weather patterns in the areas you plan to travel and how they've developed historically, even the inland sections.

Although I thought Fraser hadn't been spending as much time and effort on planning as me, it turned out I was wrong.

He'd been stealth planning for all sorts of challenges I hadn't even considered, as I was to find out as we wended our way southwards.

Dartmouth to Portland   Sunday 30th April
Distance: 56.5 nm   Time @ 5.5kn: 10½ hrs
HW Dover: (0815) and 2043   Pass Bill 8hrs 53min in.

HW Plymouth: 0208 and 1509 Pass PB from Plym. -2 to HW (-2 to -1)
Round Portland Bill Plymouth -2 (Dover +0445) ①
                              -1 (Dover +0545) ② ← 1345
① Arrive PB Dover +0445   HW (Dover -0540) ③
        =   1300 DST
② Arrive PB Dover +0545 Dover +0540
        =   1400   Portland Bill is ≈ 9 hrs into passage
③ Arrive PB = Dover -0540   ∴ Depart Dartmouth 0445
        =   2043 - 0540 = 1500   Arrive Portland Marina 1445-1530

Tides (Dover)   Boat
                    0245   kns
  -5 0315   0345   +0.6   6.1
             0545
  -4 0415   0445   +0.7   +2.5   6.2
 Depart 0445 0445
  -3 0515   0545   +0.6   6.1
             0545
  -2 0615   0645   +0.4   5.9
             0645
  -1 0715   0745   +0.2   5.7
             0745
  HW 0815   0845   -0.1   5.4
             0845
  +1 0915   0945   -0.4   5.1
             0945
  +2 1015   1045   -1.6   -3.7   3.9
             1045
  +3 1115   1145   -0.6   4.9
             1145
  +4 1215   1245   -0.5   5.0
             1245
PB +5 1315   1345   -0.5   5.0
       1345 1345
  +6 1415   1445   +0.5   47.0 ÷ 9 = 5.2
             1445
  -5 1515   1545   +1.2

Depart 0415 allowing 9½ hrs to reach PB.
Arrive PB 1345
Arrive Portland 1415-1515 approx

Photo of passage planning notes

Bangor

Belfast

Howth

Dublin

Irish Sea

Arklow

Neyland
(Milford Haven)

Padstow

Newlyn

Falmouth

Dartmouth

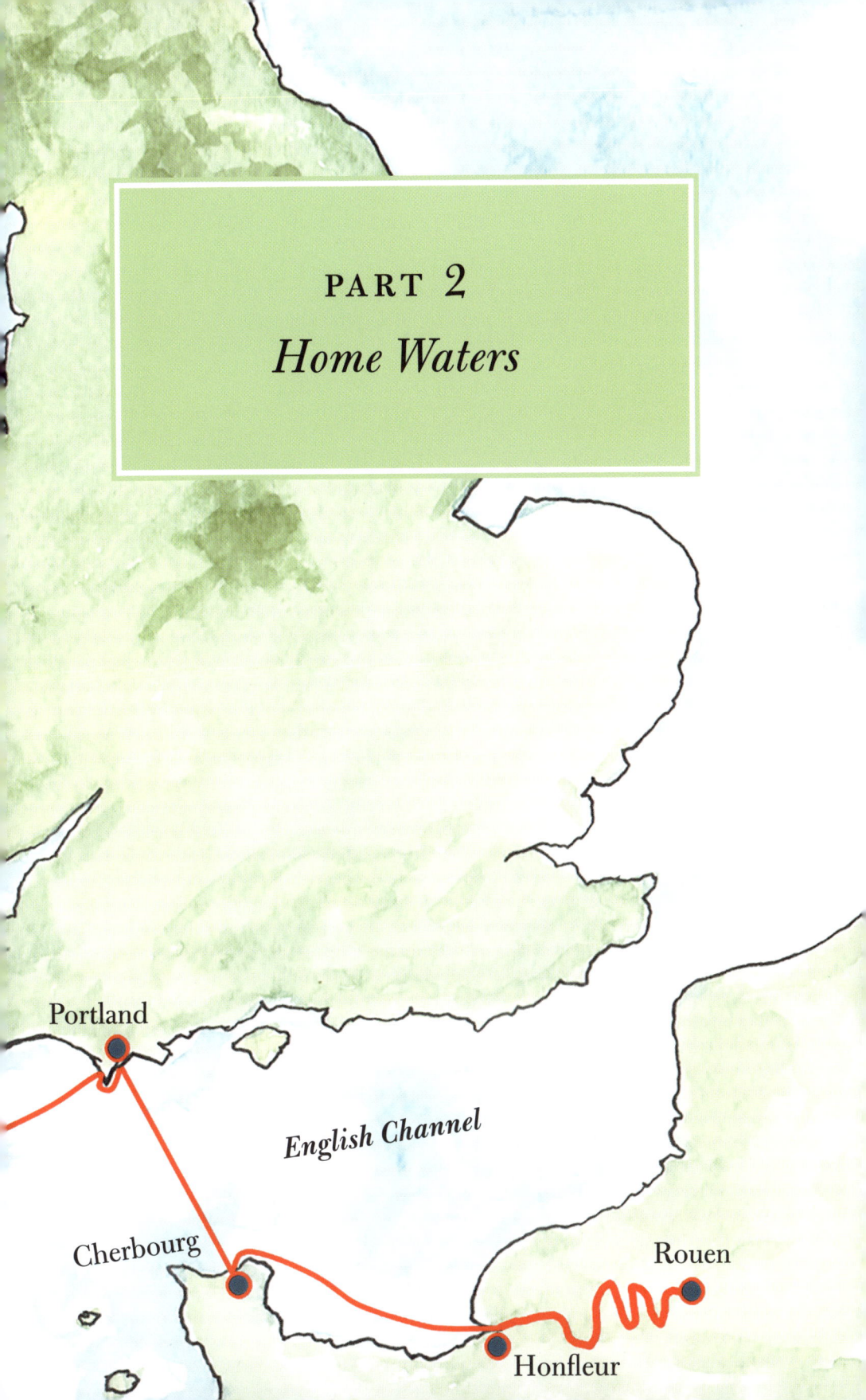

PART 2

Home Waters

Portland

English Channel

Cherbourg

Rouen

Honfleur

5

IRELAND, NORTH AND SOUTH

With the farm sold by the end of 2022 and almost all the scheduled jobs on *Barberry* completed, we embarked on some serious negotiation with our adult children regarding house and pet sitting. At last, we were free to go on our big adventure. Fraser was now panicking because it was actually happening, so planning began in earnest.

'When we set off in early May…' he began, one day in January 2023, as rain drove against the windows of the rented house we'd just moved into.

'May?' I said, startled. 'We're leaving in March, or else we'll get to the French canals too late, and the water will all be dried up.'

'Better that,' he said, 'than a pair of bloated corpses acting as a shipping hazard somewhere off Wales.'

April was a compromise we finally agreed on. I can admit, with the benefit of hindsight, that Fraser may have had a point. At least we'd packed plenty of warm clothes.

Our family gathered around us the day before we left, wishing us well and marvelling at our naivety in believing we could live together in such a tiny boat without one of us murdering the other within the first month. The fact that it was April Fools' Day was ignored, quite pointedly, by all.

However, at 0230 on the 2nd of April 2023, we slipped our lines and motored out of Bangor Marina one final time after five happy years based there.

We're not young, both of us are registered disabled, and our stamina isn't all it used to be, but that wasn't going to stop us. It does, however, slow us down sometimes as we wait for really good weather windows where younger, fitter folk might head off without a second thought.

⚓ *Family seeing us off*

IRELAND, NORTH AND SOUTH

Tidal anomaly on east coast of Ireland

Our route from Bangor to Howth was a distance of 88nm, but there's a neat tidal anomaly that gives 12 hours of fair tide in either direction. The tide swelling north-eastwards from the Atlantic splits around the island of Ireland. One branch passes to the south, surging up the east coast as far as St John's Point; the other branch passes around the north of Ireland, surging southwards to the same point. By leaving Bangor at the correct time, just as the flood begins in Copeland Sound, we were able to take advantage of this anomaly and have fair tide for almost the entire journey.

Scotland

Bangor

Northbound ebb tide for 7–12 hours

Isle of Man

Southbound flood tide for 0–6 hours

St John's Point (turning point)

Key:
— Flood tide
— Ebb tide
— *Barberry* route

Northbound flood tide for 0–6 hours

Howth

Southbound ebb tide for 7–12 hours

↟ *Tidal anomaly*

Having pushed for an earlier departure date, I could hardly complain on that dark, moonless night as I imitated a famous tyre company's mascot, so bundled up in warm clothing that I could barely bend to reach a winch. Fraser was tactfully quiet on the subject of cold as we ghosted through Copeland Sound, past the familiar beam of Donaghadee Lighthouse.

We were sped along by a south-going tide that runs for almost 12 hours, as long as you get the timing right and can maintain 6 knots boat speed in flat water. Being able to maintain only around 5 to 5.5 knots in flat water with *Barberry*, we lost the tide somewhere around Malahide. The last section of the passage was in darkness and against the tide.

Luckily, we'd visited Howth before, so we were familiar with the narrow, shallow entrance to the marina. We finally tied up nearly 18 hours after leaving our home berth.

The prevailing south-westerly winds were particularly strong in the spring of 2023, and we were effectively trying to sail south-south-west before heading across to Wales. *Barberry* has many attractive features, but sailing to windward isn't one of them. Not to worry; we spent our time in Howth usefully, with a whiskey tasting session (hic) in Dublin amongst other things.

In contrast the next leg, from Howth to Arklow, appeared relatively easy at a little under 40nm (around 7–8 hours at our cruising speed). We set off in an optimistic frame of mind, confident that *Barberry* could handle more than we could, which turned out to be true. It had been a long winter, with no sailing while we moved house and then prepped the boat. Let's just say that the tidal overfalls off Wicklow Head should always be treated with respect.

We arrived on the river in Arklow battered, bruised, a little queasy, and tied up to the long pontoon. There wasn't a lot of space, even so early in the season, but we squeezed in and slept like logs that night.

Morning brought the ripe scent of a working fishing harbour to our nostrils, and we emerged, blinking sleepily into the watery sunlight, to see a river cluttered with debris and rubbish caught around buoys and boat hulls.

As cruisers, we have found that we judge each stopping place principally on its shower and toilet facilities, closely followed by laundry and availability of shops for provisioning. We didn't stay long enough in Arklow to

↟ *Donaghadee Lighthouse*

look for shops or laundry, but I'd find it hard to recommend the shower facilities. However, the river access is straightforward when approaching from north or south, so it does make an excellent and safe place to stay for a brief stopover on passage. If approaching from the east, care should be taken when threading between the numerous banks that form a hazard along Ireland's east coast – and watch out for the pot marker buoys that proliferate in the area. These can be anything from milk cartons to small barrels. There can also be a strong tide running across the river entrance.

We were glad to cast off the following day, taking advantage of a potentially favourable wind, and point our bow towards Wales.

Lessons Learned

- Never, ever underestimate the effects of wind over tide around a headland.

- Make allowances for a long winter period of no sailing, and don't expect too much of yourself.

- Where possible, scout ahead for tricky harbour entrances. There are now plenty of online resources such as Navily to use alongside the pilot books and guides for each area.

6

WALES AND THE BRISTOL CHANNEL

This passage was the one that had most challenged our planning skills, partly because it would take us into unfamiliar waters, but also because of strong local tidal streams around the Welsh coast after a crossing of almost 90nm, which were hard to plan for.

Fortunately, we received some sensible advice from members of the Cruising Association Forum and set a waypoint 2nm SW of Skokholm, staying to the west of South Bishop and Skomer, thus avoiding most tidal overfalls and the Wild Goose race. We timed it to catch the last of the ebb, and then the first of the flood into Milford Haven. It worked, but only after a tiring period of adverse tide when we seemed to be going nowhere for hours.

Generally, we have always tried to make passage in daylight, but if that's not possible we try to set off in the dark and arrive before sunset. On this occasion, we were seduced by a promising weather window, followed by a forecast of a long spell of gales. Besides, I was keen to find better shower facilities.

In order to time the tides correctly, we left Arklow at lunchtime with an ETA in Neyland Marina of 0400, which neither of us was particularly happy about, but seemed to make sense at the time. This 16-hour passage taught us a sharp lesson: never arrive in a strange port at night, least of all one as busy as Milford. A friend had warned us we'd be confused by all the lights, and he hadn't exaggerated.

Fraser squinted into the enveloping darkness, on watch for the lights of any vessels not on our AIS.

'There's some sort of massive vessel off the starboard bow,' he called out. 'Maybe an oil rig?'

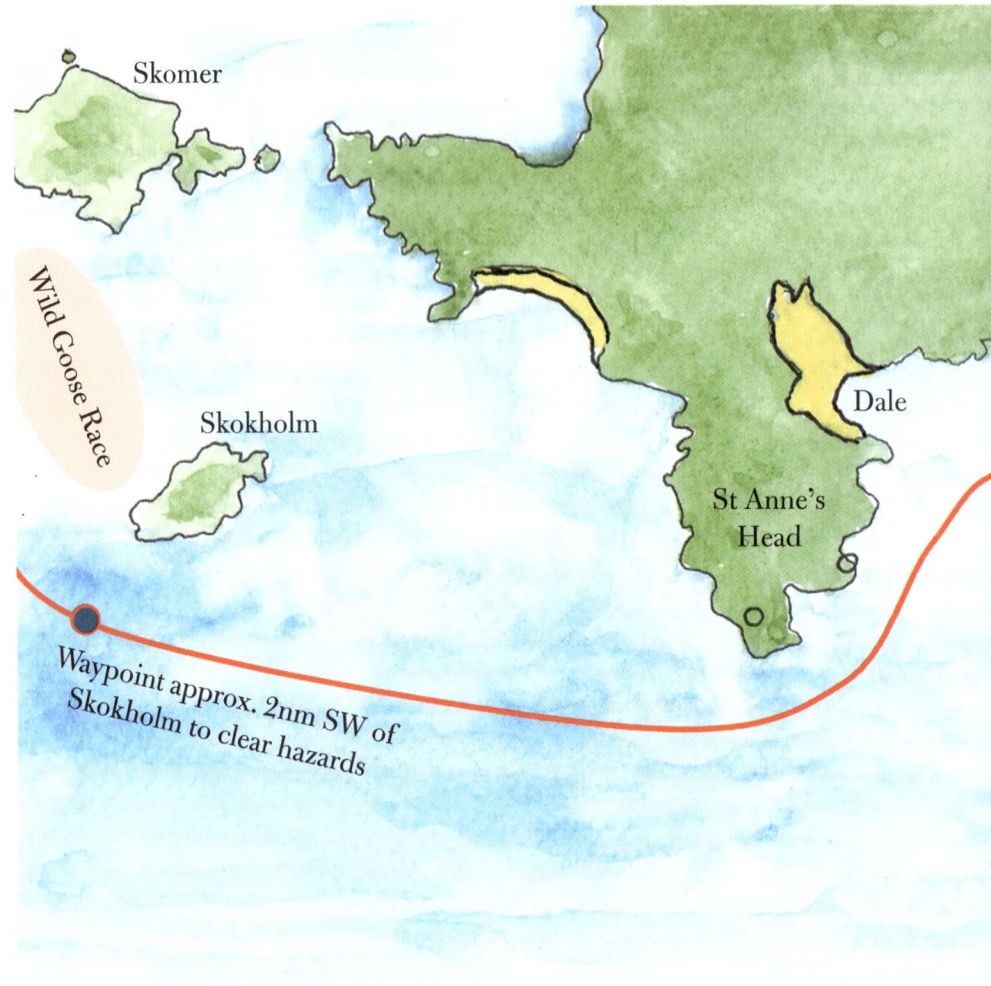

Skomer

Wild Goose Race

Skokholm

Dale

St Anne's
Head

Waypoint approx. 2nm SW of
Skokholm to clear hazards

⚓ *Entry to Milford Haven, showing main landmarks and hazards*

I zoomed in on the plotter screen and then back out again. 'Nothing showing here.'

'Well, it's moving across in front of us. You'll have to take evasive action.'

I could see what he meant: a mass of red lights, which suggested we were seeing port-side nav lights.

'It's not showing up,' I said, beginning to panic, and turning the wheel to bring us behind the behemoth, whatever it was. Why wasn't it transmitting an AIS signal?

As the threatening vessel seemed to loom closer… 'Hang on. It's not getting any closer,' I said. That's when I noticed a huge refinery inland that was marked on the chart as 'conspicuous'. It was lit up with red lights to warn aircraft.

Milford Haven
Marina

Oil refinery

Neyland Marina

Angle Bay

All the way into the estuary, port and starboard lit buoys seemed deceptive: one that looked to be miles away was actually very close but dim and mounted on a pole, and one that looked to be an imminent collision risk turned out to be an extra bright one from several miles ahead.

This wasn't our first night passage, not by a long shot, but as we sped in at 8 knots on a rising tide, we were confused by the myriad of coloured lights and movement, and beginning to believe our dazzled eyes instead of the charts.

That's when the fog rolled in, reducing visibility to less than a boat length within minutes.

Oh, and I'd failed to renew the subscription on our chart plotter, so that gave up the ghost around the same time.

Before anyone jumps on us, yes, we do have paper charts onboard, and yes, we do use them. They were of little practical use in this instance as we needed two pairs of eyes constantly on watch for pot buoys, channel markers, commercial shipping, and factories masquerading as commercial shipping. I ended up navigating using Navionics on my phone (a thing I swore I'd never do) and by eye.

The original plan had been to anchor in the bay at Dale so we could make a break for Cornwall as soon as possible, but the weather forecast drove us to seek better shelter. As it was Easter weekend by then, we'd struggled to find a berth at any of the marinas when we phoned ahead, but as we have such a shoal draught, Neyland was able to squeeze us into a shallow berth.

We almost overshot the tiny channel into Neyland Marina, but Fraser finally spotted the weakly lit starboard marker as it loomed at us out of the fog. At one point, our sounder registered zero and a mudbank appeared a few feet

to starboard, but somehow we managed to avoid going aground.

Neyland was a wonderful place to weather the storms that followed, and we made friends with a lovely sailing family who were able to share valuable local knowledge for our next leg. Oh, and the showers were great – if you remembered to put your shoes out of range of flooding, or they would float off without you.

During our stay, we kept hearing reports of storm damage and monstrous waves in Cornwall. Fraser turned paler with each report – did I mention that he suffers from anxiety?

We were in Wales for the Easter holidays so we broke out our carefully saved Easter eggs. We'd stored them in Ziplock bags, pre-smashed so they'd fit into lockers more easily. It felt surreal to be munching on delicious chocolate after the relative hardship of the previous few days but, when cruising, you take comfort whenever you can.

Neither Fraser nor I had used public transport much since our school days, so this was a steep learning curve for us, but we weren't going to waste a good opportunity to visit the delights

▼ Neyland at low tide

of Pembrokeshire. With the help of internet maps, we took buses to the West Wales Maritime Museum (wonderful place, with true enthusiasts trying to save and restore old boats), the Pembroke Dock Heritage Centre, and Pembroke Castle, where the sun finally showed its face. Until then, we'd begun to think Wales was in monsoon season as it seemed to rain non-stop.

There was a danger of staying in Wales forever after the stress of our last passage, but we did eventually make preparations to leave once we saw a weather window for Padstow opening up on the weather apps.

Timing the passage from Neyland to Padstow is ruled by tides in the Camel Estuary at the other end, as the Doom Bar (even the name gave Fraser goosebumps) shouldn't be attempted outside local HW+/- 0300 or in darkness (at least for first timers). With a 15-hour passage, that left little choice, in April, but to set off in darkness. We decided to leave Neyland at 2230 on Friday 15th April. At least we'd had a week to scout the

⚓ *Easter eggs*

Seasickness

On the subject of seasickness, Fraser has been prone to it since his teenage years in Ocean Youth Club, and it's always a concern for us when planning long passages. Since his treatment for prostate cancer he can't use some of the available remedies, such as scopolamine patches, so he's been trialling a variety of other methods to prevent sickness.

The wrist bands (acupressure) seem to help a bit, but only in mild conditions. After the crossing to Neyland, when he was nauseous but not actually sick, he invested in a TENS-type wrist device. I suppose it's a step up from the wrist bands. Even with it turned up to maximum, he could barely feel any tingling at all but when I tested it, I could feel it easily, so maybe he's too thick-skinned for it to be of benefit. It works by delivering small pulses of electric shock to the same acupressure point as the wrist bands.

For the Bristol Channel crossing, he wore the fancy electrocution device and also swallowed a couple of Stugeron tablets. He's always careful to only eat things that he doesn't mind seeing twice, so we usually heat up some mushroom soup for cold crossings and keep it in flasks. None of his prevention aids seem to help, although he still goes through the motions (as it were) for every passage. He's decided that his state of mind makes the most difference, and that everything else is probably only having a placebo effect.

Maybe that's why I rarely get seasick? I have an unsquashably optimistic nature and thoroughly enjoy every voyage. Maybe the fact that I don't expect to get seasick helps me not to feel ill. Or maybe my bright, smiley face makes my crew feel nauseous. We'll never know!

estuary and memorise the trickier sections for the way out.

The first part went well. We felt refreshed after a lazy week of tourism and were ready to be on the move again. The wind was forecast to be on our port quarter, gusting a little over 20 knots, but the sea state was slightly more of a concern, with the weather apps forecasting 2.3m swells. However, perhaps a little rashly, we went anyway.

Once out of the estuary, and into the danger area for pot buoys, we hauled out a reefed genoa, as the wind was almost dead astern. That's when things began to go wrong. The figure-of-eight knot

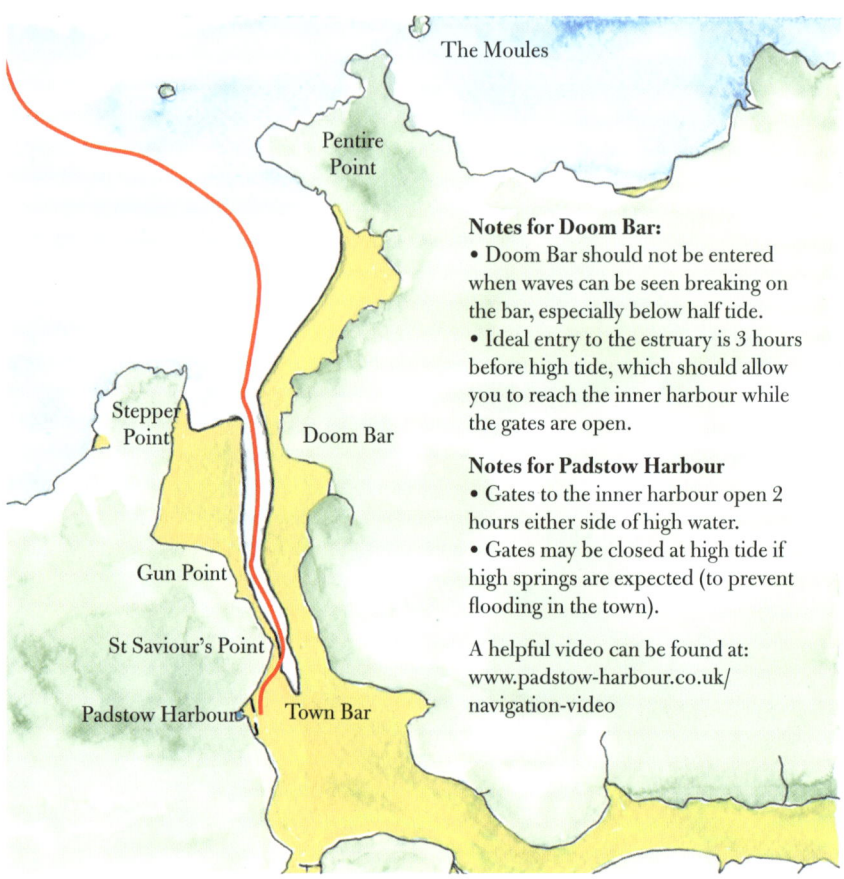

The Moules

Pentire
Point

Stepper
Point

Doom Bar

Gun Point

St Saviour's Point

Padstow Harbour

Town Bar

Notes for Doom Bar:
• Doom Bar should not be entered
when waves can be seen breaking on
the bar, especially below half tide.
• Ideal entry to the estuary is 3 hours
before high tide, which should allow
you to reach the inner harbour while
the gates are open.

Notes for Padstow Harbour
• Gates to the inner harbour open 2
hours either side of high water.
• Gates may be closed at high tide if
high springs are expected (to prevent
flooding in the town).

A helpful video can be found at:
www.padstow-harbour.co.uk/
navigation-video

⬆ *Padstow approach*

in the working genoa sheet undid
itself and the line trailed over the
side. Engine in neutral, we tossed
around in pitch blackness, still
far too close to shore for comfort,
deafened by the flogging genoa
and in danger of fouling our own
propeller. Fraser clipped himself
on and managed to go forward to
retrieve it, thankfully. After that, we
tied *double* figure-of-eights in both

sheets just to be sure.

Heading forward in the dark
seemed to tip Fraser over the
seasickness threshold. Once
he was back in the cockpit, he
became even quieter than usual,
but it took me a while to notice
because I was trying to steer us
through waves that felt far bigger
than 2.3m with a confused cross-
sea where the cliffs sent the

swell back at us. It wasn't until he started digging around in the cockpit locker for the ship's boke-ette that it dawned on me that he was in trouble.

The rest of that passage was misery for him. He eventually went below and tried to sleep, but the boat was tossing too much for him to get any rest. While I was alone in the cockpit my mobility issues made me afraid to move about the boat, even though I was lifejacketed and clipped on – I didn't want Fraser to have to do a MOB drill in the state he was in – so I jammed myself in behind the helm, grateful for the autopilot, and sat it out.

Once I became accustomed to the motion of the boat, I began to enjoy myself (while feeling guilty that Fraser wasn't). As the sun came up, silhouetting Lundy on the horizon, I realised the swells really were as big as I'd thought in the night. I estimated 4–5m, but another sailor we met later in Padstow reckoned 6m. Fraser makes similar claims about the size of fish he's almost caught.

Sunrise at sea is one of the many highlights of cruising. I did wonder, occasionally, if Fraser was still alive down there but decided that there was nothing I could do about it for now, so I continued to keep my full attention on the boat and the surrounding sea.

He resurfaced blearily when we were a few miles out from Doom Bar. 'Are we there yet?' Then he looked ahead, saw a wall of white water reaching halfway up the cliffs of Newland Island, and went even paler. 'Maybe I'll go back down for a bit.'

Padstow Harbour Commissioners have an excellent video on their website, showing the best way to navigate Doom Bar and the estuary. We were grateful for all the effort they've gone to as we finally dropped out of the rough waters of the Bristol Channel and into the flat calm of the Camel Estuary. It felt as though we'd experienced some sort of test, set for us by Poseidon, and we must have passed it because we arrived just in time for the tidal gate to allow us into the inner harbour, and then a small boat headed out, leaving a perfect space for us.

The transition from tossing helplessly on huge seas to dodging boats laden with tourists in hot sunshine was surreal. Fraser resurfaced and we took turns to dash below to peel off multiple sweaty layers of cold weather sailing gear, wishing we'd each kept a pair of shorts out of the vacuum-bagged

Lessons Learned

- Try not to arrive in a new place at night, especially after a long, cold passage.

- Remember to renew your electronic charts subscription.

- It's easy to make mistakes when you're cold and tired, especially if it's dark and/or foggy.

- After a storm has passed over, allow time for the sea state to settle before heading off.

- Check and double-check all your running and standing rigging, then check again before each passage. We had, but had somehow overlooked that almost-undone knot.

- Seasickness can be debilitating and if you're singlehanded or sailing shorthanded, you need to be prepared.

summer clothes we'd buried in a locker somewhere.

Over the next few days, a kind friend sent us some weather updates, one showing a perfect window for the Land's End passage, which I passed on to Fraser.

'No thanks,' he said. 'Let's wait for the next one.'

He was still quite shaken by his recent experience (there's a reason the Bristol Channel is often referred to as the washing machine). In the end we stayed in Padstow for a week.

↓ *Padstow Harbour*

7

CORNWALL AND THE SOUTH COAST

We spent our week in Padstow acting like good little *emmets* (from the Cornish for ants), eating pasties, seeing the sights, and catching the bus into Newquay to meet up with some old friends whom we hadn't seen in years. One of them is a former lifeboat volunteer and now works for the coastguard, so he entertained us with stories about how many hapless sailors he'd rescued over the decades.

One of his tales was about a group of rocks we would pass on our way to Land's End, The Quies. Apparently, they look exactly like a battleship from certain angles, which is how they found themselves being torpedoed by a German submarine during the Second World War.

After the unpleasantness of the Bristol Channel, Fraser was having doubts about continuing.

'I wonder how much it would cost to get a delivery crew to bring *Barberry* to Cherbourg,' he mused one morning as he munched on a Cornish pasty. 'We could stay here until they tell us it's all over, then get a flight to France.'

I'm still not entirely sure he was joking.

The passage from Padstow around Land's End is another tricky one for timing, because your departure is restricted by the opening hours of the Padstow Harbour tidal gate (local HW+/- 0200, although during springs the harbour master sometimes partially closes it around HW to prevent flooding in the town).

We left as soon as the gate opened, around 0540, stemming a flood tide of around 2–3 knots until we passed over the Doom Bar. This timing means that for the average cruising yacht, with a speed-over-ground of 5–6 knots, the tides around Land's End will always turn foul before you make it round.

In addition, for those heading south-west and then east, like us, there are only about 3 hours of fair tide around Land's End. Boats going the other way, apparently, enjoy up to 9 hours of favourable tide. Pity we've no plans to come back that way anytime soon. It's fair to say that we had plenty of opportunity to admire the Longships lighthouse as we crawled past it at 2 knots.

On passage, we usually take two-hour shifts during the day so one person gets a rest while the other keeps watch. Fraser went down below as we approached the Longships and emerged two hours later.

'Why are we going backwards?'

A rain cloud oozing along in the same direction relieved itself all over us for the entire journey, adding to our misery. By the time

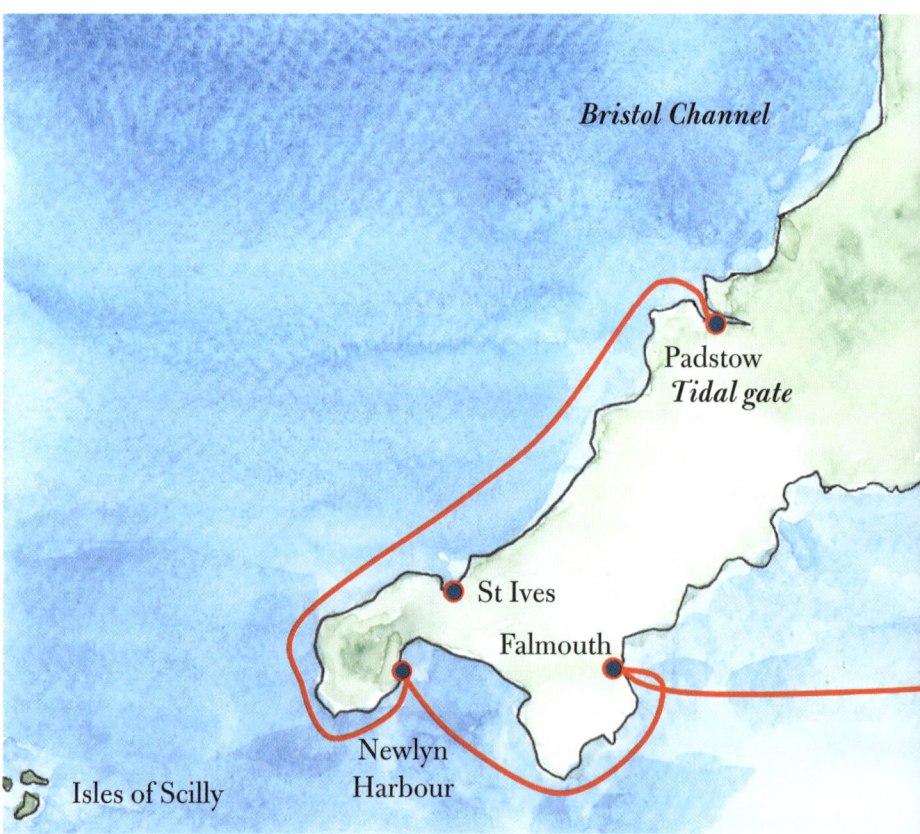

Bristol Channel

Padstow
Tidal gate

St Ives

Falmouth

Newlyn
Harbour

Isles of Scilly

↟ *Padstow to Portland*

we chugged into Newlyn Harbour, we must have looked like a pair of drowned rats.

Many people we spoke to when planning this voyage advised us to head into Penzance rather than Newlyn, but I'm glad we decided not to. For a start, Newlyn provides access at all tides, whereas Penzance has a sill, which would have restricted our departure times for the Lizard, but Newlyn also boasts a proper marina with finger pontoons, water and electricity, excellent showers, etc. It's primarily a fishing harbour, so you can expect to be tucked in between trawlers as we were, but yachts are definitely welcome. In Penzance, we'd have been rafted up, which can be a challenge for me with my mobility issues.

Be aware that dogs are not allowed in Newlyn Harbour,

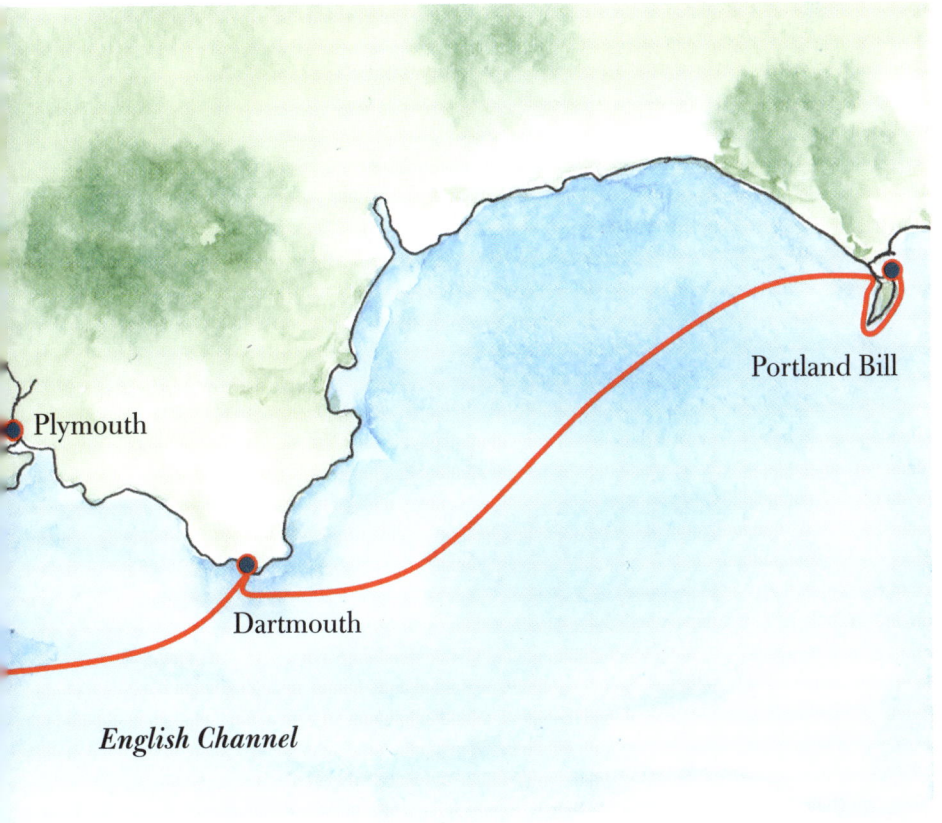

Portland Bill

Plymouth

Dartmouth

English Channel

on or off boats, because this is a commercial fishing harbour. If you're sailing with your four-legged friend, Penzance is the better option.

When we arrived in Newlyn, we intended to head off again at 0400 the following morning to round the Lizard, but when my alarm woke me at 0330, and I checked the Windy app, the forecast had worsened significantly. We have made a rule not to depart if the weather models predict winds much above 20 knots, partly because we've often found forecasts to underestimate winds and partly because we don't have the same confidence in our ability to manage the boat in stronger winds that we used to have when we were younger. The model that morning predicted 25+ knots, so we turned over and went back to sleep for a few more hours.

In retrospect, it was a good decision. We'd been thoroughly soaked on the Land's End passage and needed a couple of days to dry out. And that has absolutely nothing to do with our custom of celebrating a safe arrival after a difficult passage by downing a tot of whisky.

There are regular buses (with very reasonable fares) that can take the sight-seeing yachtie pretty much all over Cornwall. We recommend the open-top Land's End Coaster, but make sure you choose a dry day!

After bussing all over Wales and Cornwall, seeing places we might not have reached easily by car and without the worry and expense of parking, we've become converts to public transport. We even took a bus into Penzance to do our laundry on the rainiest day since Land's End. Top tip: there's a welcoming pub called The Longboat right across from the launderette, and they serve a delicious cream tea while you wait for your washer and dryer to finish.

For the first time since leaving Bangor, we broke out the folding bikes in Newlyn. There's very little storage space on a boat as small as *Barberry*, but the Brompton folding bikes are both lightweight and extremely small when folded. Fraser has an ancient one that he 'borrowed' from his mum. She bought it at one of the Boat Shows, pretty much in the earliest days of Brompton Bikes.

The second bike is a snazzy Cambridge blue electric Brompton that I treated myself to with my first big royalty cheque for my novels. You may scoff, but believe me, an electric bike is the only way

↟ *View from the top of St Michael's Mount*

I can keep up with Fraser, who competes in triathlons for fun. We cycled along the front to Penzance, parked and locked the bikes, then set off across the causeway to St Michael's Mount.

Being an impatient type, I'd got us there too early so we got slightly wet feet as we crossed. After that there were stairs, more stairs, and then a few extra stairs in case anyone was finding it too easy. The views from the top were unbelievable though. Well worth the climb (once my vision cleared, and my breathing eased enough to hear a far-too-fit Fraser pointing out landmarks in the distance). He was really enjoying his time on land.

After almost a week the weather finally settled, offering us a four- or five-day window of stable westerlies, so we decided to make a run for Portland Harbour in a series of day sails. This meant an 0530 start followed by two 0330s and then another 0530, but we were well rested and felt up for it.

When we initially planned this voyage at home, we always knew the south coast would be busy and expensive and were dreading it. Years of sailing around the north of Ireland and western Scotland can give cruising sailors an aversion to crowded anchorages and harbours. We'd always intended to get through this stretch as quickly and easily as possible, but in the end, it surpassed our expectations. On the whole it was quieter than we had dreaded, and some days we were the only boat out there. This could be due to our ridiculously early start, as it was April when we cruised this area, and the weather was still cold and blustery.

We'd hoped for a bit more help from the tide on the first leg than we actually got (neaps), so it was a slowish six- to seven-hour cruise around the Lizard to Falmouth. Looking on the bright side, no tidal overfalls this time, and a smooth crossing with dolphins sighted.

We'd booked ourselves a space in Port Pendennis Marina but needed to top up the fuel first at the fuel barge belonging to Falmouth Haven Marina. We radioed ahead and were told we'd be next after a yacht that was just finishing, so I hovered *Barberry* as close as I dared while ferries and fast motorboats skimmed by us from all directions. Just as the other yacht left and I put her into forward gear, a huge wooden gaff ketch appeared from nowhere, speeding up to the fuel barge right under our noses.

I guess might has right, because they didn't even glance my way as

⬆ *Camel Estuary from Stepper Point*

they proceeded to fill both their huge tanks in a leisurely manner while I fumed and fumed. I just needed to have to grow a thick skin, I realised. We still weren't used to sharing the seas with so many other boats, or to the faster pace of life around there.

They eventually finished and set off, apparently oblivious to my high blood pressure, and we were able to top off our tank. I think the whole fuel barge episode took around ninety minutes, of which maybe fifteen was spent filling up.

At Port Pendennis we squeezed in between a pair of beautiful yachts, each almost double our length, then checked in (*Barberry* is beautiful too, but not quite as shiny). The marina staff were friendly and helpful, and the showers were the best yet. Afterwards, we shared a delicious pizza in a restaurant overlooking our boat before hitting the sack early in preparation for another pre-dawn start. Weather apps were giving warnings of fog in the Fal Estuary, but when we woke the next morning, it was a still, clear night, so we decided to go for it and see how bad it was outside the harbour.

For early starts like this, we tend to layer up, then layer up even more, until we can't bend to untie a fender,

on the principle that it's easier to undress than dress – a bit like reefing early, because it's easier to shake out a reef than put one in. On that morning, wary of fog, we looked like a pair of Teletubbies as we grunted and panted our way around the boat.

The fog did appear, patchily, as we chugged out to sea for the 12-hour passage to Dartmouth, but at least it brought a flat calm sea. Not enough wind to sail an Optimist dinghy, never mind our hefty, long-keel lady, but we didn't really care now we had plenty of fuel.

When Fraser went off watch for a snooze, after sitting on the bow with a powerful flashlight on pot buoy watch until dawn, I had a visit from a pair of dolphins who played in our bow wave for half an hour or so before heading off to do whatever it is that dolphins do all day.

There's something uplifting about a dolphin escort. It makes us feel honoured and always seems like a good omen. We'd had at least one dolphin sighting on every leg of the journey that far except one, so there must be plenty of them around, but the excitement never really diminishes.

We passed quite close to the Eddystone Lighthouse which was, on this calm day, a magnet for small fishing boats that lit up my screen with AIS targets and kept me on my toes. Like the Longstone, passing this lighthouse, built on rocks that barely appear above the sea, filled me with awe. It seems impossible that humans could have built these impressive structures in such inhospitable places, but there they are, large as life.

Fraser re-emerged as we closed the Eddystone Rocks, a little grumpy that I hadn't woken him for the dolphins, and that's when the mist cleared, and the sun came out. We took turns to peel off a few layers, and Fraser even broke out the fishing rod, but after a frustrating time adding more and more weights to the line, he decided we were going too fast to fish. Since I refused

to slow down, the rod went away again. Maybe it would come back out in the Mediterranean.

The approach to Dartmouth was spectacularly beautiful. Fraser took photos of the castles and the picturesque rocks while I stressed about the number of boats buzzing in every direction, about pot marker buoys, about rocks, and about where we were going to tie up for the night, as we couldn't raise anyone on the VHF. We suspected that those photogenic high cliffs weren't great for VHF radios as all we got was interference every time we changed to Channel 11.

Eventually we made contact and were directed to a deep-water pontoon, Charlie Delta, where

we tied up for the night. These pontoons are basic, covered in seagull poop and empty mussel shells, with no water or electricity, and boats buzz past extremely close, but we were tired enough to sleep like the dead despite all the hubbub.

As Fraser cooked his speciality corned beef hash for dinner on the paraffin stove, we remembered that this was a homecoming for *Barberry*. She had spent the first 18 years of her life on a drying mooring (with beaching legs) on the River Dart, and was named, or so we were told, after the Barberry Brook, a tiny tributary of the river. It felt good to have brought her home for a brief visit.

On our way into Dartmouth, we'd seen how many pot marker buoys were scattered across the entrance, so we knew we'd need to be alert as we slipped our lines at 0400 in the dark. When we woke, it was to the sound of rain hammering on the cabin roof, which never brings joy to tired sailors. However, it was next stop Portland Harbour, and we had enough to worry about with Portland Bill, so a bit of rain seemed the least of our problems.

Once fenders were in and lines stowed, Fraser took up his usual position on the bow with his flashlight. We use a pair of Bluetooth headsets with microphones to communicate when we're leaving early (aka

↓ *Fraser fishing (or trying to)*

⚓ *Hitch-hiker*

Marriage Savers), so we don't have to shout and disturb other boat owners, but also because it can be hard to understand each other when we're at opposite ends of the boat.

Fraser had barely reached the bow and switched on his flashlight when he yelled into to microphone, 'Neutral!'

Partially deafened, I overshot into astern for a moment in my panic. 'Did we catch it?'

No reply.

'I think we're clear,' he finally said, but his voice was brittle with stress. The line had passed directly beneath us. Although our propeller is well protected by our long keel, and we have a rope cutter, we're always anxious about tangling in a pot marker buoy line.

We made excellent time motor sailing to Portland, and a few miles out from the Bill, we picked up a hitch-hiker in the form of an exhausted little bird who fluttered onto our chart plotter and sat staring at me for a while before investigating the hatch to the cabin, then eventually flying off. We think it might have been a female whitethroat, migrating north.

As per Tom Cunliffe's wonderful *Shell Channel Pilot*, we aimed for the thick end of the

← *Bluetooth headsets, aka 'marriage savers'*

wedge of cheese that Portland Bill resembles from the sea, but we'd made such good time that we had to hang around there for almost an hour, drifting along beneath the cliffs while we waited for the tide to turn in our favour.

We'd read many accounts of Portland Bill passages and watched numerous YouTube videos. There always seemed to be dozens of boats buzzing around it in both directions, but we had the place entirely to ourselves as we sling-shotted around. Scores of people were clambering on the rocks at the end of the Bill, and we were so close that we could have had a conversation with them if it hadn't been so windy.

It felt amazing to get another notorious passage under our belts, and we motored into Portland Marina filled with relief and pride. Two oldies with disabilities in a 40-year-old yacht, and we'd made it all the way from Bangor to Portland.

The showers in Portland Marina were warm and reviving, but as we'd arrived on a Sunday, there didn't seem to be anywhere open for dinner, so we went back to the boat for tinned hot dog sausages and pasta.

There was still one day left of favourable weather in the forecast, so the next morning, after a good night's sleep, we set off around 0630 to cross the Channel.

Lessons Learned

- Don't allow yourself to be pushed into an early departure when you're exhausted. This is especially true for those who, like us, are no longer young and/or have disabilities.

- You won't always have the tide with you. Be patient, and it'll turn eventually.

- Check weather before a passage; forecasts can change significantly between going to bed and the alarm clock ringing.

- The pace of life on the south coast is far faster than we were used to.

- Pot marker buoys are the bane of a sailor's life.

- Portland Bill doesn't leap out and eat boats, as long as you're careful and treat it with respect. Research and timing are everything.

- With Portland Bill, the advice is either take the inside passage as we did, or take an extremely wide passage to avoid ferocious tidal overfalls.

Pot buoys

Once, many years ago and in a different boat, we picked up a lobster pot between Coleraine and Rathlin Island and only discovered that we'd been towing it when we went astern, and it popped up behind us. I'd been wondering why my tidal calculations were so far out. Unfortunately, that pot caused some damage to our shaft seal, and led to a leak that might have sunk the boat, so we've probably been left a little traumatised!

However, we escaped this time and once we were in deeper water, Fraser came back to the cockpit to defrost. A steep chop accompanied the driving rain, so it was a relief to see him safe, tucked up beneath the sprayhood.

Portland Bill, inside passage to avoid tidal overfalls

8

THE ENGLISH CHANNEL AND NORTHERN FRANCE

The weather, after a slightly foggy start, was perfect for a Channel crossing. We had a steady 14–15 knots of wind and could easily have sailed the whole way on starboard tack, but we were so close to our goal that we both felt a strong sense of urgency, so we used the engine to add a couple of extra knots to our speed. It took us a little over 11 hours before we motored between the massive Second World War fortifications that form Cherbourg's outer harbour wall.

We suspect there are many sailors who keep their boats in Cherbourg and never sail outside the harbour. There's certainly plenty of room to enjoy a few hours of tacking to and fro', dodging ferries and commercial craft, and we passed several big yachts seemingly quite happy to sail around inside the harbour. Hard to blame them, since the tides outside sweep past at an incredible rate.

We found a snug berth on Q (P and Q are the visitor pontoons), and it's lucky we were mentally prepared for the French marinas, with their extremely short, narrow pontoon fingers and lack of cleats on the end. Instead, there's a metal loop on the end of the finger, which makes setting up springs a bit of a challenge, even on tiny little *Barberry*. Bigger boats must have even more trouble. The finger pontoons are also quite unstable, so Fraser stepped off with extreme caution with the lines and managed to avoid bouncing himself off again!

To be standing on French soil after such a challenging voyage (for us; others would probably have found it easy) was an incredible feeling. We met the crew of another UK boat, also crossing the Channel for the first time, and they felt the same sense of euphoria and disbelief.

Because we have Irish passports, we didn't need to jump through quite the same hoops as most UK sailors. We'd sent the Border Force form in online, and emailed the Cherbourg form to the Frontier Police, following it up with a visit to the station the evening we arrived, to show our passports and to deliver the hard copy of the form.

It's worth noting that although social media and forum scuttlebutt (naval slang for rumour or gossip, which took place around the scuttlebutt, or water cask) suggests that the frontier police will regularly visit the marina to check papers, we saw no evidence

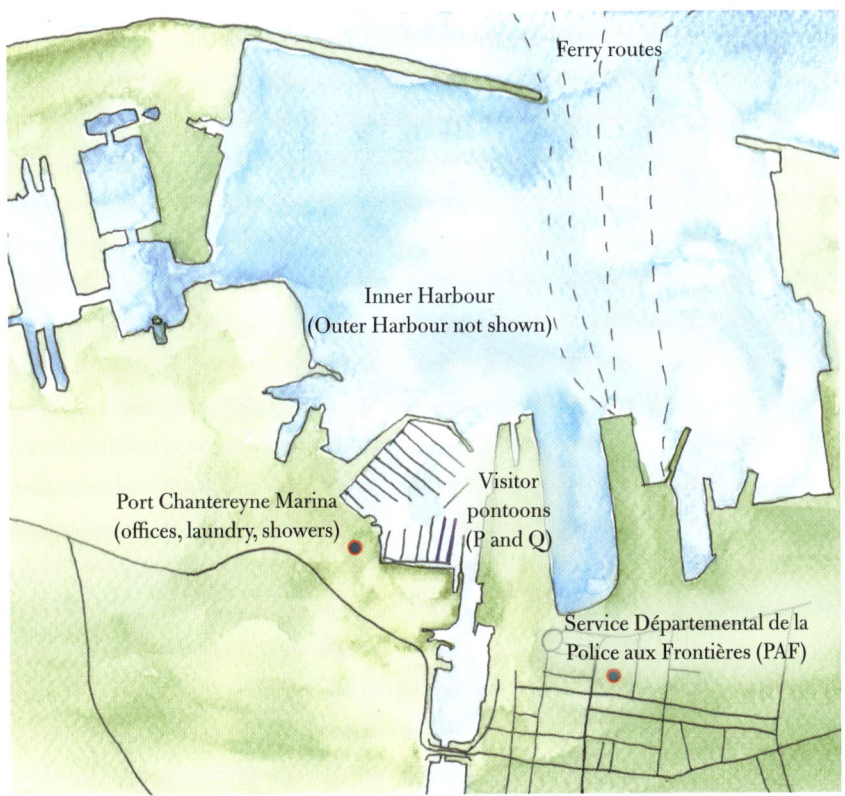

Ferry routes

Inner Harbour
(Outer Harbour not shown)

Visitor pontoons
(P and Q)

Port Chantereyne Marina
(offices, laundry, showers)

Service Départemental de la
Police aux Frontières (PAF)

⚓ *Cherbourg Inner Harbour and marina*

French finger pontoons are often much shorter than the ones UK sailors are used to. They can also be quite narrow and wobbly.

⬥ *French-style finger pontoons*

of that, and it's a good 20-minute hobble to the station to present yourself in person. They do expect you to visit them as soon as you arrive, and they won't let UK folks check out of the country the night before a passage, as our friends hoped to do. They had to present themselves at the station at 0600 for an 0700 departure for the UK.

When we arrived at the building where our internet map placed the Frontier Police, we could find no entrance. We walked most of the way around the building before finding a small unmarked door that was unlocked. A scary-looking policeman, in full uniform and sporting a Hercule Poirot moustache, demanded our papers. We handed them over, trying to explain (in atrocious French) that we didn't speak very much French.

After glowering at the passports for a few minutes, he barked something unintelligible at us and disappeared into a back room. By then, too tired to remember any of my schoolgirl French, I was ready to cry and expecting to be thrown into a jail cell.

Very often they don't have cleats at the end (or even middle), but instead may have a loop of steel (shown in red here).

After a long wait (probably not as long as it felt), a small plump man in shirt sleeves and braces popped out of the back office, brandishing our passports in the air.

'You are Irish,' he said, in perfect English. 'We do not need to see your papers!'

On our walk back, both limping and limp with relief, we passed several restaurants. Most were extremely busy and the menus in French were too much for our tired brains to translate. At last, we spotted a burger place and headed inside. At least we knew what a burger looked like.

We should have realised, when the waiter asked how we would like our burgers cooked (*bien cuit, moyen, à point, ou saignant*) that this was going to be unlike any burger either of us had tasted before. The food was out-of-this-world delicious, and exactly what we needed at that moment in time.

The marina at Cherbourg is a good place to spend a few days. There are numerous excellent restaurants and shops an easy walk away, but the office, showers, toilet facilities and laundry are maybe a 10-minute walk from the pontoons (at least for me). The showers and laundry are excellent, and the staff pleasant and helpful. I think they spoke pretty good English but respected my attempts to communicate in French with patience, giving me hints when I forgot a word or made a mistake.

The next leg was a 14-hour sail to Honfleur, and as we'd already experienced the power of the tides along that coastline, we planned for it carefully. It was a beautiful sail initially, racing along with a perfect wind and a strong tide, but once past the last headland, the wind died away so we motored the rest of the way into Honfleur across a glassy, calm sea, past silent monster cargo ships crouched above their reflections. We watched their AIS avatars on our plotter carefully, and kept an eye out for smoke from funnels, but none of the sleeping giants awoke so we passed in peace.

The tide was in flood again as we entered the channel leading into the River Seine, so we made good speed, sticking as advised (counter-intuitively) to the wrong side of the channel because although there is deep water in most places just outside the channel to the north, mudbanks leave zero room for manoeuvre outside the channel to

Small craft keep to north side of the channel

Main (commercial) river traffic passes port to port in marked channel

↟ *Entrance to River Seine and Honfleur*

the south. We did have to dodge commercial vessels a couple of times so we were glad we'd followed the advice.

Turning from the fast-flooding Seine into the lock at Honfleur was an interesting challenge. The tide swirls muddily along the south bank, and the entry channel to the lock looks far narrower in real life than on the charts or on internet maps. Also, it was dusk by then and the visibility wasn't great. We could see black piles leading up to the lock, but not the lock gates themselves. At least, we could see a

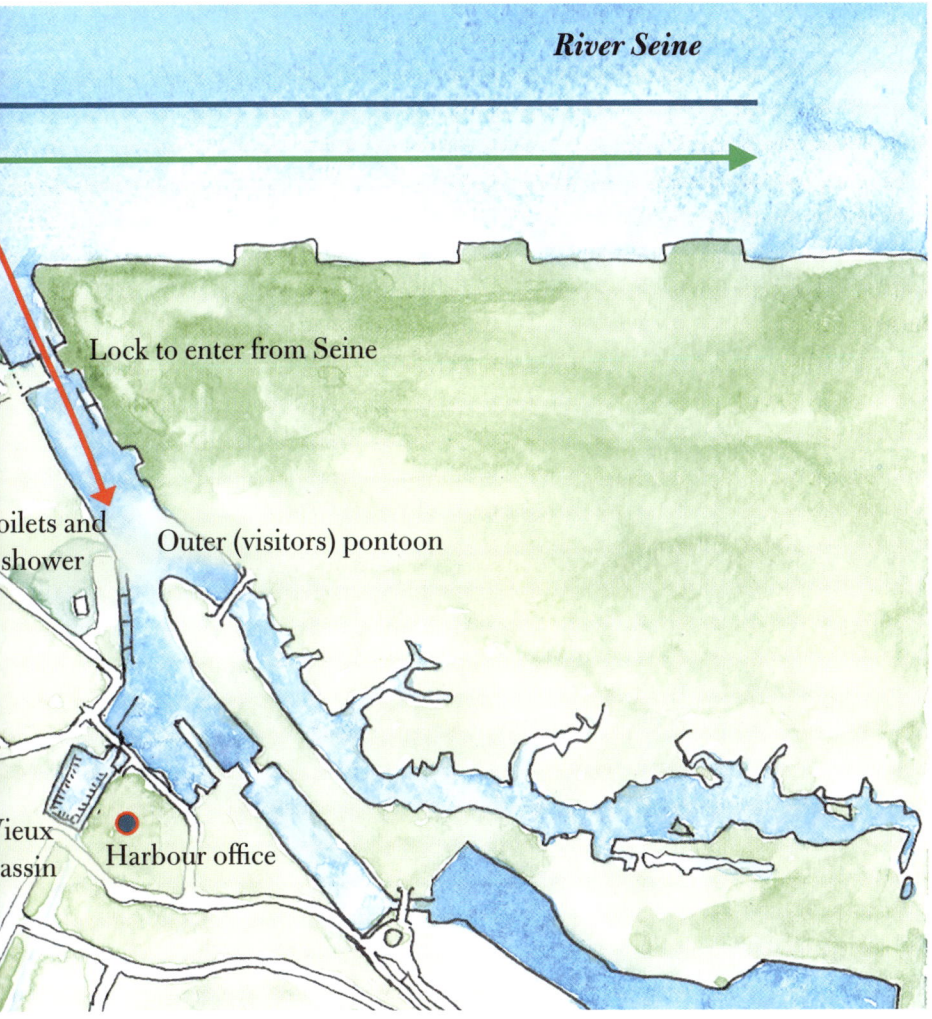

River Seine

Lock to enter from Seine

oilets and shower

Outer (visitors) pontoon

Vieux assin

Harbour office

gate but couldn't tell if it was the one at our end or at the far end. We'd radioed the lock keeper (*éclusier*), so we knew he was expecting us, but had he opened the gates?

After a dramatic handbrake turn across the tide, *Barberry* was dragged from side to side by fierce eddies as I tried to line her up with the lock. By then, we'd seen the green light, but the far gate still looked awfully close. This lock is wide but fairly short, so we had to stop quickly, having gunned the engine to counteract the currents, so Fraser could drop a line from our midships cleat over the middle rising bollard of three.

Once the boat was safe, the *éclusier* closed the gates and filled the lock: sanctuary. We were still a little shaky as we motored over to the Ponton de Jardin, the outer visitor pontoon, and rafted up alongside a lovely, friendly Dutch couple.

Honfleur is an incredible place to stay and in some ways, I wish we could have spent longer there to explore. The single full day we had was rainy, yet still the ancient streets and market stalls charmed us. We visited a café and enjoyed the most expensive snack imaginable (Scottish Fraser was affronted at having to pay so much for a tiny cup of coffee and a dry croissant), then we were persuaded to buy a miniscule amount of tomato paste from a market stall at a cost of €20. Restaurants abounded, overflowing on to the narrow streets, and American voices were all around, drowning out the locals.

Still, the clock was ticking, and we knew we had to move on. We radioed the *éclusier* for advice about depth outside the lock, and prepared to leave that Sunday morning, slipping lines at 09.15 in misty dampness.

The lock out was uneventful – until the gates opened to reveal thick fog outside. I was too busy being nervous about the cross-current to second guess myself, but as soon as we were in the main tidal Seine and flying along at 12 knots over the ground, I began to realise that this might have been a mistake. We didn't see the first bridge until we were beneath it, and it passed over us faster than I'd have thought possible.

Radar and AIS were invaluable as we motored upstream with water droplets misting our eyebrows and hair. The tide was so powerful that we couldn't have turned back if we'd tried. Fortunately, the fog was a local effect, and we soon emerged into better visibility.

We'd expected the lower Seine to be built up and industrial, but instead we passed through idyllic countryside with ancient, half-timbered houses, white chalk cliffs, grassy terraces and, above all, trees. So much native forest. This became a theme as we continued through France: mixed deciduous woodlands everywhere, interspersed with close-cropped grassy hills. I've never seen anything like it anywhere in the British Isles.

And birdsong. We were accompanied the entire route by a varied chorus so loud we could easily hear it over the engine. We saw a fat otter on the riverbank (which we later learned might have been a coypu), and innumerable species of wild birds, including kingfishers.

It was a dream journey, and we really didn't want it to end, but eventually we sped into Rouen, still managing 7 knots on the last of the flood tide (which gets later the further upriver you go), and into a wobbly berth in the Bassin St Gervais. We'd somehow managed the passage in a little over 7 hours.

Lessons Learned

- The English Channel isn't scary at all after the Irish Sea and Bristol Channel.

- French finger pontoons require a new approach and an agile crew.

- It's worth brushing up on your French before you go to France.

- Don't judge a burger by its cover.

- Always carry out a visual check of the conditions outside before leaving a safe harbour.

- The Seine to Rouen is beautiful but tides run very fast indeed. Timing is critical as there is nowhere safe to stop en route.

↓ *Entrance to Honfleur Lock at low tide*

PART 3

An honorary barge

9

FROM SAILBOAT
TO MOTORBOAT

Once in Rouen, we needed to turn *Barberry* from a sailing boat into a motorboat by removing her mast to allow her to pass beneath low bridges. The Bassin St Gervais is the last point at which a masted boat can safely pass, so that's where we stopped.

We had booked ahead with Lamanages, the yard recommended by Gordon Knight in the Cruising

↟ *French inland waterways*

⚓ *Flying Colours in a lock on the River Bann in Northern Ireland circa 2009*

Association's Guide, *Through France via the Inland Waterways*. It was excellent advice: the yard was efficient and the crane man, Antoine, spoke good English. The crane was booked for Tuesday at 1000 and we arrived in Rouen on Sunday, giving us ample time to prepare the mast for lowering.

When I say *us*, I mostly mean Fraser. He's a retired professor of biomedical engineering, and he brings the same calm, logical approach to boat jobs as he did to his research into joint implants. Without fuss, he disconnected the through-mast wiring and together we flaked sails (a process that

Crane and mast in Rouen

always makes me grumpy), then removed the boom, spinnaker pole and whisker pole. He taped all the bottle screws to mark their position and labelled each stay before slackening off the tension.

Many years ago, we brought a different boat up and down the River Bann from Lough Neagh to the sea several times, carrying her masts onboard (she was a ketch). It made us realise that the mast, being a lot longer than the boat, can be a liability in locks if the current swirls the boat around. There's danger of damage to either end as both stick out, making them vulnerable to rough stone walls. These overhangs also make it harder to find marina berths or alongside berths, as your overall length is greater than without the mast.

The other downside to carrying your mast is the head-bumping hazard: you have to either duck under the mast or climb over if you need to reach the other side of the boat, which you frequently do, especially as you approach a lock. This makes moving around the boat slower and more difficult, and increases the risk of someone falling in.

After some helpful advice from Jonathan of the YouTube channel *Sailing Options*, we had the name of a reliable company to use, Boat Loads (boat-loads.com). A few phone calls and emails reassured us that our mast would be collected by Nigel, returned to the UK for safe storage, and then transported down through France to meet us in Port Napoléon.

Taking down your mast is always an anxious procedure, but we'd been through it the previous year when we replaced all *Barberry's* standing rigging, so it was still fresh in our minds. The hoist at Lamanages is quite new-looking with a nice, shiny yellow mast crane attached, and Antoine operated it with a remote control that allowed him to shimmy up the mast to place the strops while making adjustments. He then directed Fraser to undo the stays in order until the mast was freed from the boat. All the while, rain pounded down, finding gaps in our waterproofs.

We removed the bottle screws to take them with us, having had a previous bad experience with a different boat when they hadn't been secured for transport, and several came loose and were lost. Once the mast was on its wheeled trestles, we returned *Barberry* to her wobbly berth, looking naked without her mast, then trotted back to the boatyard with sail bags, boom and other spars.

The marina has a couple of wheelbarrows for the use of patrons, but I think we were lucky to get one because after that day I didn't see either of them again. It's a long enough walk from the marina to the yard, especially when you're balancing so much stuff on a wheelbarrow. It took us a few runs to get all the gear transported that needed to go with the mast. We opted to have Nigel transport *Barberry's* sails and spars along with the mast, leaving us a bit more room in the cabin.

We had thought about bringing materials such as bubble wrap along with us to protect the mast for transport but decided they'd take up too much space. Luckily a skip in the marina provided plenty of old cushion foam for padding (Fraser is often attracted to skips) and we dug out some spare canvas and an old sail bag from *Barberry's* stores to wrap

⌃ *Mast wrapped and ready to be transported*

the delicate masthead fittings. We removed the Windex, then loosened the fittings (VHF aerial and LED tri-light) so we could tape the aerial down the side of the mast to protect it from damage. We also taped the stays to the mast steps to prevent chafing and padded all the vulnerable bits. The spreaders, like the bottle screws, came back to the boat with us.

After sending Nigel photos of the finished project, and a list of all the items he needed to transport, we went back to the boat for a serious siesta. Despite Antoine's unfailing cheeriness and support, it had still been an exhausting procedure.

We staggered back, wellies sloshing with rainwater, hair dripping, like a pair of drowned rats. My usual technique for boarding from a finger pontoon is to grab the stays and swing myself up and over the guardrails. This time I reached, my hand swiped thin air, and I almost overbalanced on the unstable pontoon. Boarding without standing rigging for support was going to need a rethink.

Fraser had spent time during the previous cold Northern Irish winter thinking through the challenges we'd face. He'd devised a clever system that allowed us to retain the main boat radio (using the spare aerial) instead of resorting to a handheld VHF. We called it the mini mast, and I hung our French courtesy flag from it.

Fraser made the mini mast by attaching the spare VHF aerial to an old mooring aid, creating standing rigging out of bits of string, then ran the cable down through the deck fitting into the splitter, which meant we also had AIS. This made a huge difference as we could see other vessels approaching around a bend and also if the lock ahead was empty of commercial traffic or if we'd have to wait a while.

One of our other concerns, apart from our water draught, was *Barberry's* air draught. Our radar arch (useful for attaching burgees for the Cruising Association and Women on Barges, as well as our tiny Irish tricolour) was difficult to measure with a plumb line because the act of standing on the pushpit to hold the line resulted in the stern dipping, thus reducing the air draught.

We estimated her air draught was a conservative 3.2m and as the lowest tunnel or bridge, according to published data, would be 3.4m, we reckoned we'd be okay. Of course, that published clearance is at the highest point of an arch in most cases, and our arch has a flat top carrying the full height almost to the edges of the boat. In an emergency, we knew we could unbolt the arch and lower it down, but luckily, we didn't need to.

A *vignette* is needed for travel along the French inland waterways. This is a licence that gives you the right to use the locks and to tie up to the bank (where suitable) for free. We bought ours online (approximately €235 for two months), which is now the only option, and a staff member in the *capitainerie* in Rouen kindly printed it out for us and even laminated it so we could display it in a window.

The *vignette* also allows the user to access the full support of the VNF (*Voies Navigables de France*), the official body that maintains canals and employs the *éclusiers*. The VNF these days is underfunded and overstretched in terms of manpower and facilities. Despite this, virtually every member of the VNF we encountered was polite, helpful, and tried their hardest to keep the system running.

The balance of opinion in the *capitainerie*, when we sought advice, was that it should take us about four days to reach Paris, so we phoned ahead and booked a space at the Arsenal Marina for arrival on 13th May. We also asked advice about tides and the best time to leave the marina, as we could find nothing online or in our guidebooks or pilots that mentioned this. No two sources of information agreed, so we decided to trust local knowledge, with some interesting results.

Lessons Learned

- Forward planning is essential. Fraser had prepared the long boathook and the mini mast before we left Bangor.

- You can't have too many long lines aboard if you plan on going through locks. We used old halyards.

- Don't buy shiny new fenders before cruising inland waterways.

10

PREPARING THE BOAT
FOR INLAND WATERWAYS

Sailors spend most of their lives trying to avoid contact with hard objects such as walls. Once you enter the inland waterways, land is all around you and much of it is bounded by rough concrete walls, so a steep learning curve ensues.

One priority is to have enough fenders. Ours were pretty old and

Barberry

tatty, but there seemed no point in replacing them just before the canals and that turned out to be a wise decision.

Use as many fenders as you can manage along both sides of the boat to protect the gelcoat from rough concrete, but extra protection is needed fore and aft, for when the boat swivels around in a lock. We have big ball fenders that we tie each side of the stern to protect it when the boat rotates in a lock (this is almost inevitable). We also deployed Big Red, a huge, cylindrical inflatable fender that we inherited from a friend, and set him up on the port bow, because we prefer to go port side-to where possible due to our prop kick. We'd have liked at least another ball fender to protect the starboard bow, but in the end it was fine. One of us could always protect it by pushing the boat away from the wall with a boat hook.

Once a lock is filled, the water is often almost up to the edge of the concrete, so fenders tend to float up, rendering them useless unless you can find a way to prevent it. We

✦ Big Red, our secret weapon

used a fender plank on each side to hold the fenders down. It also protected the fenders themselves to a degree from the rough walls.

The fender boards (we brought two) were secured by two lines tied to the guardrails, just like the fenders, but they sat outside everything so they ended up between the fenders and the walls. Ours were old scaffolding planks that Fraser drilled holes in for the lines, and one of them later became our *passerelle* in the Med.

Another essential is a good long boathook. We have several onboard, but the best one for the locks was a super long (3m) composite one that we stored along the coach roof. It's still useful for gathering up slime lines in the Med (*See Remembering how to Sail section*). It is also useful as a depth gauge, as Fraser has marked a line on it at 1.2m.

Lastly, you need at least four long lines. These need to be long enough to reach up to the bollards in a deep (4m+) lock and back down to your deck again. You need a line each side on the bow and one each side on the stern. In some locks, we were able to get away with a single line each side attached to the midships cleat and passed around a pole or bollard in the lock wall. This

technique should be used with caution as it provides far less control when turbulence tries to swing the boat.

Lessons Learned

- Forward planning is essential. Fraser had prepared the long boathook and the mini mast before we left Bangor.

....

- You can't have too many long lines aboard if you plan on going through locks. We used old halyards.

....

- Don't buy shiny new fenders before cruising inland waterways.

11

A LOOK AT LOCKS

A lock is a system to move water traffic from one level to another, either upstream or downstream. The steeper the gradient, the higher the density of locks and in especially steep sections, there can be flights of locks, one after another.

French locks are managed by *éclusiers* who usually work for the VNF, or one of the big power companies who run the hydro-electric plants associated with huge locks on the big rivers such as the Rhône, eg the CNR (*Compagnie Nationale du Rhône*).

PK markers

Another useful aid to navigation on the inland waterways is the use of PK markers (*Point Kilométrique*) which are shown on the river and canal guides and occasionally can be seen between the trees on the banks as you travel. They're a good way to keep track of how far you've travelled and how far remains to the next stopping place or point of interest. They're (surprisingly) one kilometre apart.

How do locks work?

On rivers, a lock usually bypasses a drop in level such as a barrage or weir, so you should be prepared for strong currents in the approaches. There are usually plenty of warning signs saying not to follow the main flow of the river and the guidebooks will show which side of the river to expect the lock. Even on canals, water can stream out from the sluices and create a current.

A lock chamber is a stone – or concrete-walled passageway with a row of low bollards along both edges or set into the walls.

Traditional lock chambers have pairs of hinged wooden gates either end, with sluices that can be opened to let water through. In giant locks on big rivers, this looks very different as you'll see later, but the principle is the same.

↟ *Blue and red poles in a lock can be used to start the cycle*

A boat enters a lock once a green traffic light is shown, the gates close behind her, water in the lock is raised or lowered to the same level as the next pound, and then she leaves via the set of gates ahead of her.

When the sluices open to fill the chamber (boat travelling upstream), turbulence can be severe at the upstream end of the lock, close to the gates, so care must be taken as the boat rises with the water level until the lock is filled.

Once it's safe, the upstream lock gates swing open to allow the boat into the next reach, which can be 4m or more above the one it has just left.

If you're heading downstream, the whole process is reversed. The lock needs to be filled before the gates can open to let a boat in, then it empties with the boat inside and opens the downstream gates once the lock is empty. When going down there is less turbulence, but be aware that there may be a concrete sill beneath the upstream gates. This is hidden by the water until the chamber begins to empty.

Communicating with the lock keeper

On major rivers, you need to radio ahead to tell them you're coming, how far away you are, and in which direction you're travelling. This presupposes a certain fluency in French which not all of us possess and can be made even more challenging by poor VHF reception from a low-level aerial/handheld. I often resorted to phoning the lock, using the number from the river guide. The

conversation was easier that way. Note: the French never use the word 'over' on VHF, making radio chat even more confusing.

In smaller waterways, locks were mostly unmanned, so radioing ahead wasn't necessary.

Be aware that commercial traffic always has right of way over leisure traffic in all rivers and canals. Locks in big rivers are usually enormous in all dimensions, leaving a private boat feeling very small indeed inside one (and also guilty about the amount of water used if you're on your own in there).

The *éclusiers* in these giant locks are usually sitting in a raised tower that allows them to see the entire lock and approaches. They have full authority over who enters the lock and in what order. Don't assume that if you arrive when the lock is clear and the gates are open that you can just mosey on in. You must check with the *éclusier* because they might be aware of a giant push-tow barge on its way, but out of sight from your position. You won't be allowed to enter until the commercial vessel is in and safely secured.

If you do follow a commercial vessel into a lock, remember there can be concrete ledges (sills) beneath the surface at the upstream end of the lock, so if you're going

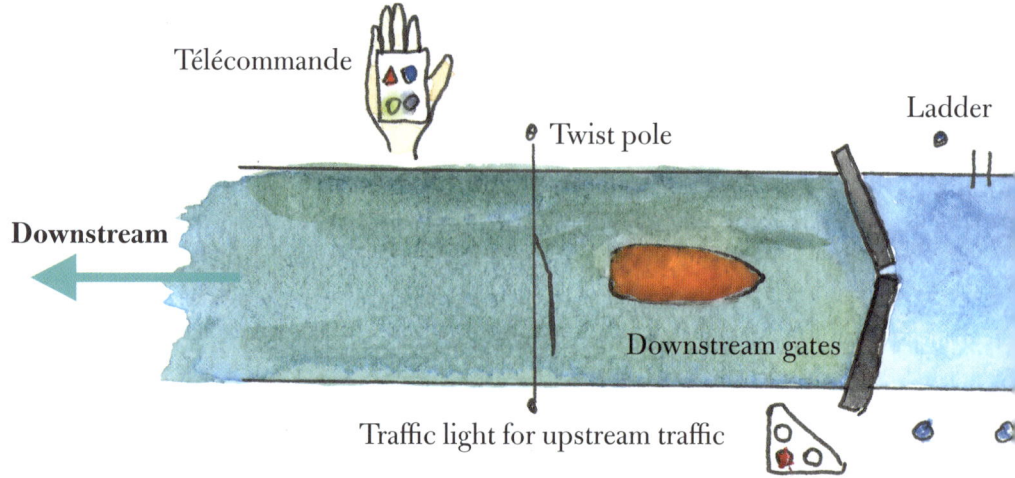

Télécommande

Twist pole

Ladder

Downstream

Downstream gates

Traffic light for upstream traffic

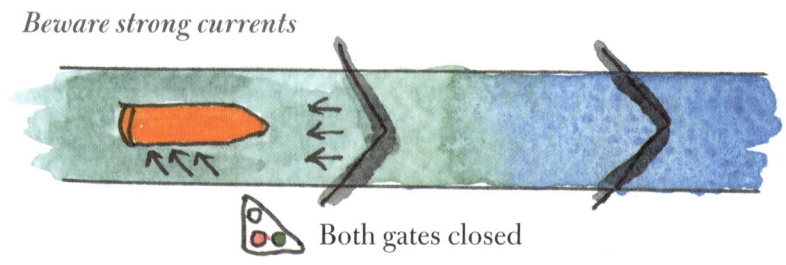

Beware strong currents

Both gates closed

1. Lock emptying

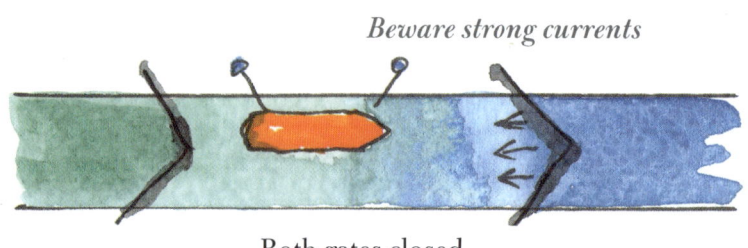

Beware strong currents

Both gates closed

3. Lock filling

↟ *Major components and function of a typical French lock*

Red and blue operating rods

Traffic light for downstream traffic

Lock chamber

Upstream gates

Upstream

Bollards   Ladder

Operate lock by:
a) Raising blue pole, or

b) Pressing correct button
on Télécommande

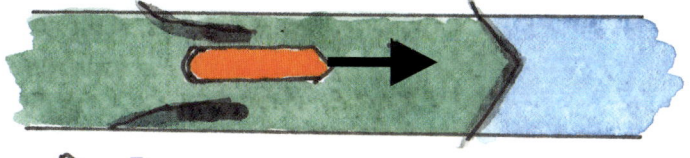

Downstream gates open

2. Boat enters lock

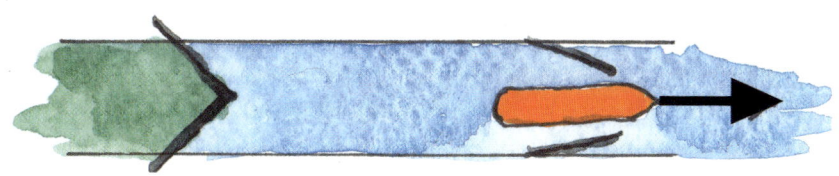

Upstream gates open

4. Boat exits lock

⬆ *Concrete sills can be hidden beneath the water until the lock is empty enough to see them*

downstream, look out for guidance in the form of warning signs. Hopefully the *éclusier* will tell you if you're in a dangerous position, but they're human and you might be hard for them to see, just a tiny spec behind the barge.

Also, be aware that when a commercial barge operator engages gear, his propeller wash can throw a small boat around. Stay attached to the bollards in the lock wall and alert with boathooks at the ready until the water settles instead of trying to follow a *péniche* straight out.

⌃ *You can feel very small inside these deeper locks*

⚓ Barberry *waiting for a big lock*

⚓ Barberry *behind a péniche inside one of the larger locks*

Traffic lights

Locks, tunnels and lifting bridges all have a traffic light system that tells the boater what is happening (if anything).

Two red lights:
Lock not currently available to you. May be a long wait. May need to radio/phone VNF.

One red, one green light:
Lock is preparing for entry. Be ready to move off.

Flashing orange light:
Your presence has been noted (by sensor or remote). Wait for red or green lights.

One red light:
Lock not currently available, but will be soon. There might already be a boat in the lock.

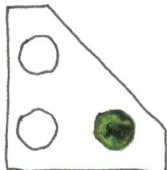

Green light:
The lock is open and ready for you to enter.

↟ *Traffic light operation*

- Always wear lifejackets in locks.

- Never tie up to a ladder.

- Always watch out for, and give way to, commercial traffic.

- Expect some turbulence on approach to a closed lock gate and inside the lock chamber. Also from prop wash if you're behind a commercial vessel.

- Keep clear of concrete sills that may be hidden under water (descending).

- A really long boat hook and long lines are invaluable.

- Watch out for fenders and fender board lifting when descending inside a lock.

- Be polite to *éclusiers*: they are responsible for efficient passage for all vessels, not just pleasure craft.

- In smaller locks, bollards can be almost impossible to see once inside the chamber and hard to drop lines around, even with the help of a boat hook (ascending).

- Protective gloves should be worn when handling lines, especially in locks.

A LOOK AT LOCKS

Types of lock

SMALLER LOCKS

Manual

These are often found on British inland waterways, but less common in France (we didn't see any). Often, an *éclusier* might travel by van or bicycle to cover several locks in their area. If you do come across this type, it's considered good manners to offer to help if you have sufficient crew to do so safely. Also, don't expect the *éclusier* to catch your lines for you. They might, if you're lucky, but it's not really a part of their job. If they do, thank them. Profusely.

⚓ *Many moons ago, manual lock operation on the River Bann (2009)*

Semi-automatic

Twist pole locks, aka perches

As the name suggests, these are operated by a crew member twisting a rubber pipe that dangles from a wire across the canal. We never discovered if they should be twisted clockwise or anticlockwise, so Fraser tried both ways until the traffic light changed.

For this type, I would place the bow of the boat as close to the dangly pole as possible so Fraser could reach it.
– This often involved steering the boat near to the edge of the waterway where the weed was thickest.
– Then reducing speed to a near-stop to give him time to manipulate the pole without having to sprint aft along the side deck while hanging off the end of it.
– Once he'd let go, the pole would rattle along *Barberry*'s length until I was able to give it a shove away from the boat, so it didn't hit our radar arch.

The aim was to manage it first time and not to have to go back for another go, although that did happen from time to time when the traffic lights didn't change.

⚓ *Typical twist rod*

⚓ *Fraser on deck, ready to twist the pole*

Automatic sensors

These detect the passing of a boat on the approach to a lock and set the cycle in motion. We didn't see any of these, but I guess the only way to know if you've been detected is to wait for the traffic light signal.

It's advised not to go too fast on the approach to any lock, because these sensors can miss a boat if it passes too quickly.

Remote control (*télécommande*)

For some stretches we were given one of these little boxes to operate the locks.
– There would be a sign on the bank as we approached the next lock with a picture of the remote control. Once you reached that spot, you'd press:
- the blue *Montant* button for travelling upstream,
- the green *Avalant* button for travelling downstream.

– It's very important to remember which way you're travelling, as pressing the wrong button prepares the lock for a boat coming the other way which jams the entire system until either:
- a boat appears from that direction
- or a man in a van turns up to reset it. Best not to ask how I know this.

– Once inside the lock, you can press the paler blue *Bassinée* button which starts the lock cycle. It took us an embarrassingly long time to realise this, and we kept on trying to push up blue poles for quite a few locks before someone took pity on us and told us about the other button.

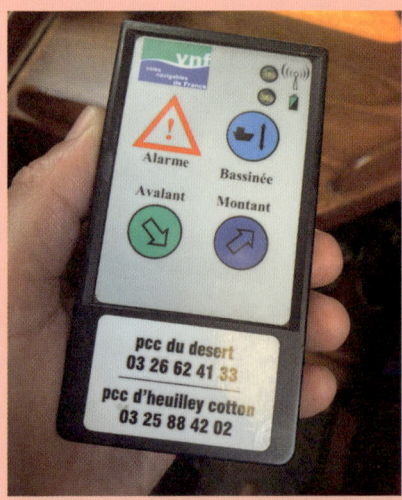 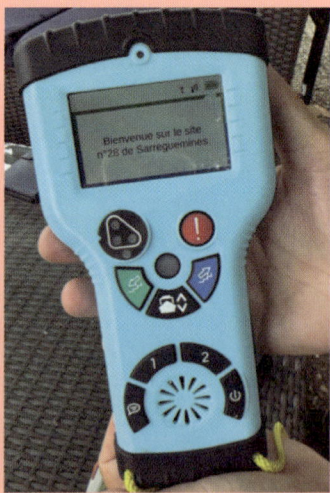

↟ *Télécommande. Note: a new version of the télécommande unit is currently being trialled in France (right). Photo credit to Jonathan Shanks whose blog, europeanbargee.com, is also filled with useful information*

Push pole locks

Once inside, the lock can be operated by pushing up the blue rod. These are often slippery with algae and can be stiff to operate. That's probably because we were the only idiots trying to use them in that part of the system. Everyone else was using the remote control.

There is also a red rod, which is pulled down to raise the alarm in the event of an emergency, such as a man overboard. Having said that, the poor old VNF is so overstretched I feel that the casualty would have either drowned or climbed out unaided long before any help arrived. Perhaps the red rod freezes the lock's operation, shutting the sluices so the casualty doesn't get swept to their death under water by the powerful currents. I'm glad to say we never needed to use a red pole, so we can't say for sure.

UNUSUALLY-SHAPED LOCKS

V-shaped locks

Some locks have a V-shaped cross section with sloping walls. Most of these also have floating pontoons that you can tie up to just like a finger pontoon in a marina. The pontoon goes up or down as the lock fills or empties, making this type much easier than they appear at first glance.

It's wise to keep an eye on your lines in case anything snags or the floating pontoon jams. Be ready to let out line and fend off with a boat hook in case of emergencies.

↟ *In a V-shaped lock, there is usually a floating walkway/jetty with cleats instead of bollards along the top edge*

Locks with rounded sides

We didn't encounter any of these, but they do exist. This is where carrying your mast becomes a real headache as it's hard to prevent it impacting on the curved walls.

BIGGER LOCKS

These are operated by an *éclusier* who sits in a tower and communicates by VHF radio with waterway users. Their word is law! Always wear lifejackets on approach to and inside locks. It's common sense to wear a good lifejacket in a lock anyway, but the *éclusier* may not start the cycle until they see that all crew members are wearing them.

The locks on the Rhône can be more than 20m deep and are long enough to allow passage for the biggest commercial vessels. Once inside an empty lock, it's like being at the bottom of a deep well. In these deep locks the bollards are usually set into the walls of the lock.

TYPES OF BOLLARDS

Golden rule: *never use a ladder to secure your boat in a lock. They're not designed to take the weight of a boat being thrown about by turbulence, and if you break the ladder, the lock becomes unsafe (someone falling in can't climb out).*

Pole

A vertical pole runs from the top of the lock to the bottom. A line (or lines) are passed around this pole and back to the boat again, secured to a cleat.

Pros:
• You don't need to move the line from one bollard to another.
• You can often get away with a single midships line.

Cons:
• The poles may be spaced well apart as they're designed for commercial vessels.
• The poles can be slimy or (worse) rough with plant growth that catches the line and stops it moving freely, especially if it's under load. Be prepared to release the line or slacken it if it jams. Carry a knife to cut it if necessary.

⚓ *Fraser with line around a pole and using a boat hook to stop it getting jammed*

A LOOK AT LOCKS

Floating

The bollard travels up and down with the water level.

Pros:
- You don't need to adjust your lines constantly.
- You can often get away with a single midships line.

Cons:
- The mechanism sometimes squeals as metal slides against metal. In a deep lock, this can be deafening.
- The bollards are usually spaced far apart.

⊼ *Floating bollards*

Stepped

The bollards are fixed in place above each other (not always in a straight line, but sometimes staggered), so as the water rises or falls, the crew must remove the line from one bollard and move it to the next. In this case, it's always worth having a second line secured so the boat is never completely free.

Pros:
- At least you can see these bollards and they're not out of sight on the wall above you.
- You can often get away with two lines amidships (fore and aft) around one bollard.

Cons:
- Lines can slip off the top of a bollard as the angle changes. They can be quite slimy.
- Moving the line(s) from bollard to bollard can be quite exciting, especially if there's turbulence.

⚓ *Stepped bollards. Fraser has a second line ready to throw over the higher bollard so he doesn't have to take the lower one off until the boat is secured*

12

THE TIDAL SEINE AND PARIS

We spent a total of three nights in Rouen, setting off on Wednesday 10th May at 1400, just before low water (*marée basse*) according to local knowledge. For the first mile or two we seemed to have at least 3–4 knots of current against us, so we referred back to the internet to check tide times. Nothing had changed. Total inconsistency between sites, with a variation for high tide in Rouen that almost covered the entire range of the 24-hour clock.

We came the closest to an argument that we'd been since setting off: Fraser wanted to

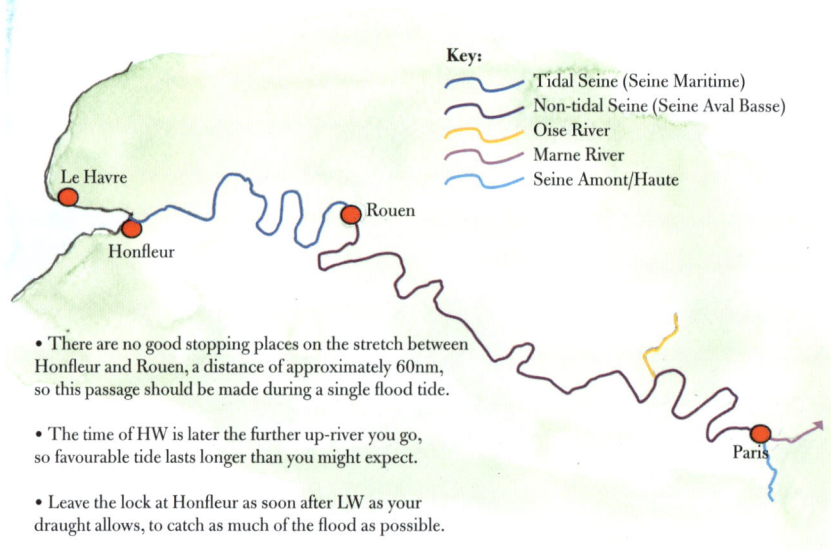

Key:

— Tidal Seine (Seine Maritime)
— Non-tidal Seine (Seine Aval Basse)
— Oise River
— Marne River
— Seine Amont/Haute

Le Havre
Honfleur
Rouen
Paris

• There are no good stopping places on the stretch between Honfleur and Rouen, a distance of approximately 60nm, so this passage should be made during a single flood tide.

• The time of HW is later the further up-river you go, so favourable tide lasts longer than you might expect.

• Leave the lock at Honfleur as soon after LW as your draught allows, to catch as much of the flood as possible.

↑ *The Seine from the sea to Paris*

⚓ *Hotel barge*

turn back and I wanted to keep going. Fortunately, while we were debating, the tide turned (at exactly the time predicted by our wise local guides) and we began to make better headway. There was still maybe 2 knots against us, but it didn't feel as if we were going backwards any more.

We'd set ourselves a target for that day of passing through the first lock, Amfreville, a distance of around 25 miles; despite the slow start, we managed that easily.

We tried to set up routes on Navionics on our phones so we could transfer them to the plotter, but it took ages to twig why it kept on saying it couldn't calculate a route. We still had it set up for a 15m air draught! Once we'd sorted that, we could lay in routes to follow and even use the autopilot to steer on the wider sections, easing the burden of hand steering much of the time.

However, we noticed that the automatic course often went along the wrong side of the river (even though the crossover places were clearly marked by arrows on the electronic chart, so it should have known better), and on more than one occasion, it wanted to take us the wrong way along an arm of the river where it divided around an island, or under the wrong arch of a bridge.

Despite its shortcomings, the plotter was still more of a help than a hindrance, but you do need to keep your wits about you and follow the clearly marked river signs instead of trusting the gizmo. One of us was always at the helm, ready to knock off the autopilot and hand steer. In fact, we hand steered at least half the time, possibly more, because of other boats. Our CEVNI revision helped us with markings on bridges and along the river.

There wasn't as much river traffic as we expected. Several *péniches* (big steel barges) and floating hotels passed us in both

↓ *A typical barge, fully loaded*

directions, but we kept to the edge of the channel to leave them plenty of space, and soon stopped getting stressed about them.

We spent our first night on the non-tidal river at Poses, tucked into a *Barberry*-sized space (with nothing much to spare at either end), right outside the tourist office along a bank shaded by trees and sheltered by an island. Dinner was eaten in the cockpit: fresh baguette, cheese and salad, washed down by a glass of wine. We slept like a pair of corpses after the noise and bustle of Rouen and awoke to birdsong and the sound of goats bleating as they browsed on the thick vegetation of the island about 30m from us.

The tourist building had lovely clean showers, toilets, etc, which we sadly didn't discover until we were just about to slip lines for a long day of motoring to our next overnight stop at Port de l'Ilon.

That was a long and tiring day. We had set ourselves only two locks to pass through: Notre Dame de la Garenne and Méricourt. Fellow Cruising Association members Tim and Karen had gone ahead of us and were kind enough to warn us of repairs under way to the Méricourt lock, resulting in no bollards on the port side to tie up to. We were grateful for the advice, as we nearly always try to go port side to. In our turn, we passed on the information to Tony and Sue who were following a few days behind us and whom we'd met in Rouen.

At each lock that day we experienced delays of anything from 30 minutes to more than an hour (although it seemed to last forever) while we waited for commercial vessels to pass through.

Holding station near the confused currents from the *barrages* (weirs) next to each lock can be challenging, especially

⬆ A Barberry-*sized space at Poses*

⚓ *Méricourt Lock was under repair in 2023 so we could only tie up starboard side-to*

when there's a huge barge leaving the lock from the opposite direction, and another huge one hovering behind you, waiting to go in ahead of you.

At the second lock, we were directed to follow a *péniche* inside and tie up behind her. That was fine, because it was a very big lock so there was enough room for Fraser to drop a line around a bollard, but the *péniche* took up the entire width. However, when she put her engines in gear to

↓ *Fraser demonstrating his 2-line technique*

move off, the wash tossed us all over the place and made steering difficult. Not sure how I managed to exit the lock without bouncing off the walls the whole way along, but the luck of the Irish held, and we escaped unscathed, with another lesson learned.

This might be a good time to explain our lock technique. I helmed and Fraser handled lines (we've done it this way since my decreasing mobility made me a liability on the side decks). I aimed to stop the boat next to a bollard, depending on the lock. Bigger locks with floating bollards, or poles, were very easy, but most of the ones we'd used so far had stepped bollards placed about 1.5m apart (vertically) inset in the wall. This meant that, with a water rise of perhaps 4–8m, you needed to move your line from bollard to bollard before it disappeared beneath the water.

Fraser quickly learned that it's safer to have a second line attached to the centre cleat, so he could secure the higher bollard with the second line before releasing the lower one, thus reducing the risk of us floating off helplessly if he missed.

We had five cylinder fenders on each side of the boat and fender boards at the widest point. Ball fenders (set quite high) and Big Red protected the hull from impact as the boat slewed around in the current when the lock filled.

In the first lock, I spent ages with my finger constantly stabbing the bow thruster button to keep the bow off the wall, but I eventually realised that the fenders did the job perfectly well, plus we both worried in case debris got sucked into the bow thruster tunnel and jammed the prop.

Once the lock had filled and we had a green light, Fraser flicked his line free and pushed us off sideways with a boathook so I could motor out with minimal contact against the slimy walls. After a lock, there's often a crossover to the opposite bank from the one you entered, and sometimes, a queue of vessels waiting to enter the lock you've just left, which can be confusing. When you cross the river above the barrage (after an upstream lock) the current tugs at you until you're clear again.

Our boat speed reduced a mile or two before each lock and increased again at the other side, which I put down to the currents from the barrage. Overall, we probably averaged 4–5 knots SOG (speed over the ground). The current even in non-tidal rivers can be significant. Once in the canals we would face speed limits, but on the Seine any limits were far higher than *Barberry* was capable of achieving, so we didn't need to worry.

The operators of commercial barges are a friendly lot and always returned our waves. They seemed to appreciate that we had a right to use the waterways too, and that helped us feel a little less guilty about getting in their way on occasion!

We have a set of Fluviacarte guides (I think these are now out of print, and have been replaced by Breil guides), some of which we bought but most of which we had been given thanks to the generosity of a couple of fellow sailors from Bangor, Gill and Del (*SV Lofna*), who did the journey in the opposite direction a few years ago. Their notes in the margin were also helpful! The guides are extremely useful, once you get the hang of reading them. We drew in a few new bridges as we passed by, but on the whole, they were pretty accurate.

The second day out of Rouen was exhausting. We'd covered over 44nm by the time we arrived late and frazzled at Port de l'Ilon, a lovely little marina in an old quarry just after the Méricourt lock. We arrived at 1930, just too late for the *capitainerie*, which closed at 1900 and wouldn't open until 0900 the following day. We found a free finger pontoon and tied up, but it was too wobbly for me to risk leaving the boat with my poor balance, so I stayed onboard.

We intended to fill up with fuel as we left early the next morning, but unlike their sister marina in Rouen, these pumps weren't self-service and required an attendant, so we gave up. We put a €20 note for the overnight berth in an envelope through their letterbox, with our details and contact number, based on the cost of the marina in Rouen, but we found out later that it should have been €13. Still, better too much than too little.

That day (Friday), we covered another 41nm, including two more locks (Andrésy and Bougival, both of which were straightforward with no waiting around) to tie up for the evening at the *halte nautique* of Rueil-Malmaison. This was a nice, neat pontoon capable of housing 3 or 4 *Barberry*-sized boats. No water or electric, but numerous restaurants close by and shops an easy walk away. Fraser took a solo trip to the local boulangerie and came back, ridiculously pleased with himself, with some delicious pastries and a fresh baguette. He speaks very little French but managed by pointing at all the yummy stuff and saying, '*Deux*'.

Commercial traffic

Péniches are commercial barges carrying freight along the waterways. They're still a common sight in France and often house entire families. We frequently saw *péniches* with the family car loaded on the aft deck, behind the accommodation section. They were historically designed to fit the Freycinet gauge, so 38.5m long, 5.05m wide and 1.6m draught.

There are also even bigger commercial barges, sometimes consisting of one or more dumb barges pushed by a single motorised unit (a push-tow barge). These do not meet the requirements of the Freycinet gauge and can only pass through the bigger river locks.

Commercial barges vary in size, but when one goes into a lock in front of you, there can be little room left behind it. We also encountered chains of barges, either towed traditionally but more commonly push-tows where the manned pusher is behind the dumb (non-motorised) cargo vessel and pushes it along. They're a magnificent sight as they pass, heavily laden and with a white moustache of a bow wave.

Although commercial barges like this often have shallow draught when unladen, they can be very deep when they're filled with a cargo of wheat or gravel, so they will be restricted to the deepest part of the channel. This must be remembered at all times, so be ready to move across to give them room, especially on bends or narrow reaches.

Also, never assume that where a barge goes, you can safely follow. Unladen they can draw less than 1m, better than most cruisers.

Hotel boats are another commercial user of the waterways. These behemoths can be as long as 110m and as wide as 11.4m. For comparison, they could fit 11 and a bit *Barberrys* into their length and 3.5 in their width, so a total of 38 *Barberrys*. We only saw these on the bigger rivers.

On the canals, vessels are limited by the Freycinet standard for lock size, allowing *péniches* up to 38.50m x 5.05m to pass through. The Canal du Midi is an exception to this rule, as well as some of the smaller, less frequented canals and waterways.

I'm sure hotel boats are a wonderful way to cruise the waterways in luxury without the stress of finding stopping places or supplies, but from the perspective of the *plaisancier* (pleasure boater), they seem to be taking over all the pretty towns we'd love to have stopped at. Many old stopping places for private craft have now been turned over to hotel boats, including jetties that would have taken half a dozen private boats for a night but are now reserved for hotel boats only.

I can see the advantage to the French towns: hotel boats bring in hundreds of people, in theory buying from the local shops and eating in the local restaurants, but we've sat and watched them many times and it always seems that passengers go ashore for a walk about, look at the pretty buildings, then return to the ship for their evening meal and drinks. How much benefit do the towns really gain from their stay?

Whatever your feelings about hotel boats, the golden rule for all pleasure boat users is: Always give way to commercial traffic. After all, they have a living to make and we're just *plaisanciers en vacances*.

↟ *Péniche stopping place complete with a ramp to crane the family car off the boat*

It had been a hard few days since leaving Rouen, but we'd broken the back of the journey to Paris and had only left ourselves around 25nm (and one lock, Suresnes) to reach the Arsenal Marina on Saturday, when we were booked to arrive. The last stage into the city was memorable for scores of houseboats of all shapes, sizes, and states of dilapidation moored along both sides of the river.

If you ever follow our footsteps (and those of many other sailors-come-river boaters), I must recommend the Arsenal Marina. It's a lovely place to stay and is close to all the main attractions of Paris. The staff are helpful, facilities some of the best we'd found, and the marina itself feels as if it might have been here at the time of the French Revolution. According to Wikipedia, the Arsenal was established by Napoleon Bonaparte in 1806, between the Place de la Bastille and the River Seine. It became a harbour for private yachts and trip boats and has gradually evolved to its present-day form.

The marina is entered by a lock from the Seine, on the right bank (our left as we headed upstream) just after Île Saint-Louis and Île de la Cité, which houses Notre Dame de Paris (Quasimodo not sighted, despite our best efforts). The marina operator speaks good English and can be reached on VHF CH9.

The highlight of our experiences thus far (and there had been many, many highs) was motoring through the centre of Paris, right past the Tour Eiffel, Place de la Concorde, Musée de Louvre and Notre Dame de Paris. Okay, navigating in the choppy water around trip boats of all shapes and sizes, including enormous, fat tourist barges and hop-on-hop-off ferries, is complete madness, but totally worth the stress.

Even with a listening watch on VHF CH10, as required, I found it almost impossible to follow the rapid French being spoken, and it took us a while to notice that someone was calling, 'Bar-berie, Bar-berie'. It was just a pontoon boat taxi, telling us that he planned to overtake us before the next bridge.

We managed to keep going, as per the rules of navigation in Paris, which don't allow for stopping to rubber-neck at the sights, but still took some photos. The bridges themselves are glorious and not to be forgotten. It would be easy to

➤ *Motoring past the Eiffel Tower was a surreal experience*

Lessons Learned

- Planning and preparation make life easier. We'd researched this trip so thoroughly that we were well prepared, making both de-masting and managing locks straightforward.

- Guidebooks can get it wrong, especially if they're older editions, but so can chart plotters.

- Four days from Rouen to Paris is pushing it; five would have been more comfortable.

- It's absolutely worth staying a few days in Paris, but book into the Arsenal Marina well ahead of time.

- Speaking French is a huge advantage, and I'm not sure how we'd have coped if neither of us had any knowledge of the language. As it was, my schoolgirl French was barely sufficient.

- Even if you have a deep-draught boat, Paris is easily achievable and worth the effort.

↑ *Locking into the Arsenal Marina, in the heart of Paris*

miss them as a tourist unless you took to the river, so we certainly forgave the packed tourist boats for taking up the entire river, then turning in front of us.

We probably appear in hundreds of holiday snaps as cameras tried to capture the Eiffel Tower with us in the foreground, grinning like loons and waving to all the (other) tourists. I like to believe that our little Irish tricolour on the radar arch cut us some slack: *'C'est juste l'irlandais fou!'*.

We spent a week in the Arsenal Marina, making time for tourist visits. We visited all the usual sights, including the Eiffel Tower, and one slightly less usual one: the sewer museum, beneath the streets of Paris where they used to roll giant stone balls through the tunnels to clear blockages like in the Indiana Jones films. We did enough walking that week to make up for four solid days of motoring from Rouen, during which we barely left the boat.

⬆ *Sewers beneath Paris: not as smelly as we expected*

THE TIDAL SEINE AND PARIS

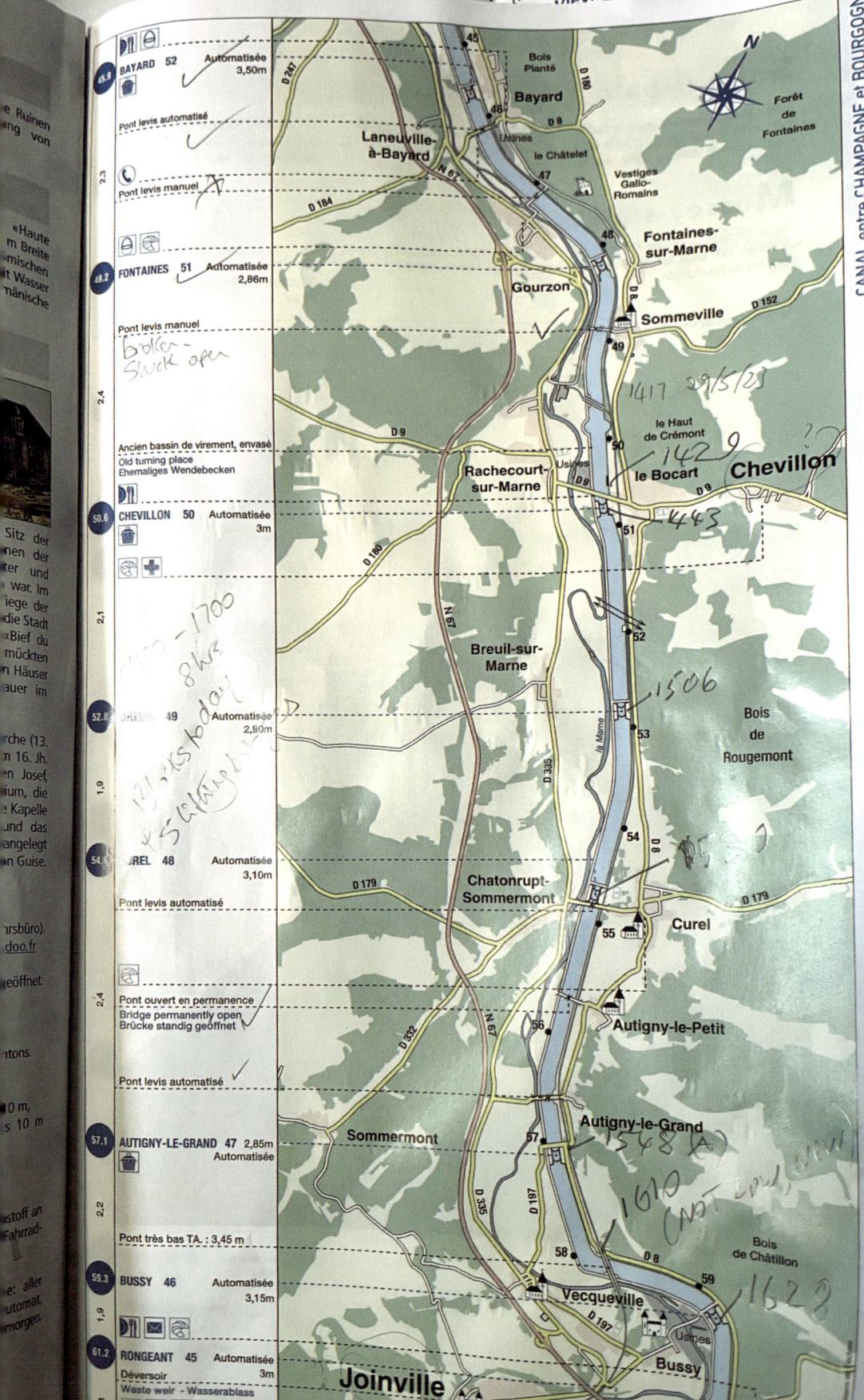

13

MARNE-CHAMPAGNE

We had originally intended to head south-east from Paris along the Loire-Saône route (See sketch at beginning of Chapter 9), but a couple of seasons of drought, coupled with heavy use by *plaisanciers*, had a negative impact on water levels. We were advised in no uncertain terms by friends, by the admirable women in the Women on Barges Facebook group (WOBs, as we call ourselves), and by fellow members of the Cruising Association that even with a 1.2m draught, *Barberry* was unlikely to get through using that route.

In Rouen, we had chatted with the owner of a Golden Hind (another well-known Maurice Griffiths design with similar draught to us) who had attempted that route a couple of times over the last few seasons, but he'd been turned back each time by the VNF due to shallow water.

So, a quick change of plans had us turning left after Paris and heading up the Marne River. This route loops north and east before joining the River Saône, then the Rhône and would eventually carry us to the south coast at Port St Louis du Rhône where we would hopefully meet up with our mast.

The few locks we'd met on our journey so far had seemed easy enough, but as soon as we'd turned off the Seine onto the River Marne, we met a lock that represented the beginning of a steep learning curve.

As I've mentioned before, our *Fluviacartes* (guides to the waterways in three languages, except when they forget to translate from French) are quite out of date. According to ours, the VHF frequency for the first few locks was

← *Our ancient Fluviacartes have several layers of notes from previous owners as well as our own scribbles*

CH20 but they have since changed to CH19. After several abortive attempts to contact the *éclusier*, we just hovered outside in the hope that he'd notice us and let us in, which he did, eventually.

Then there was the Saint-Maur tunnel, 600m in length, with a lock at each end. That was a new experience for us, and I'll swear the entrance decreased in size the closer we got to it. The tunnel was fine, once we were inside, and our 3.2m air draught cleared it easily despite the arch carrying its height almost across the full width of the stern.

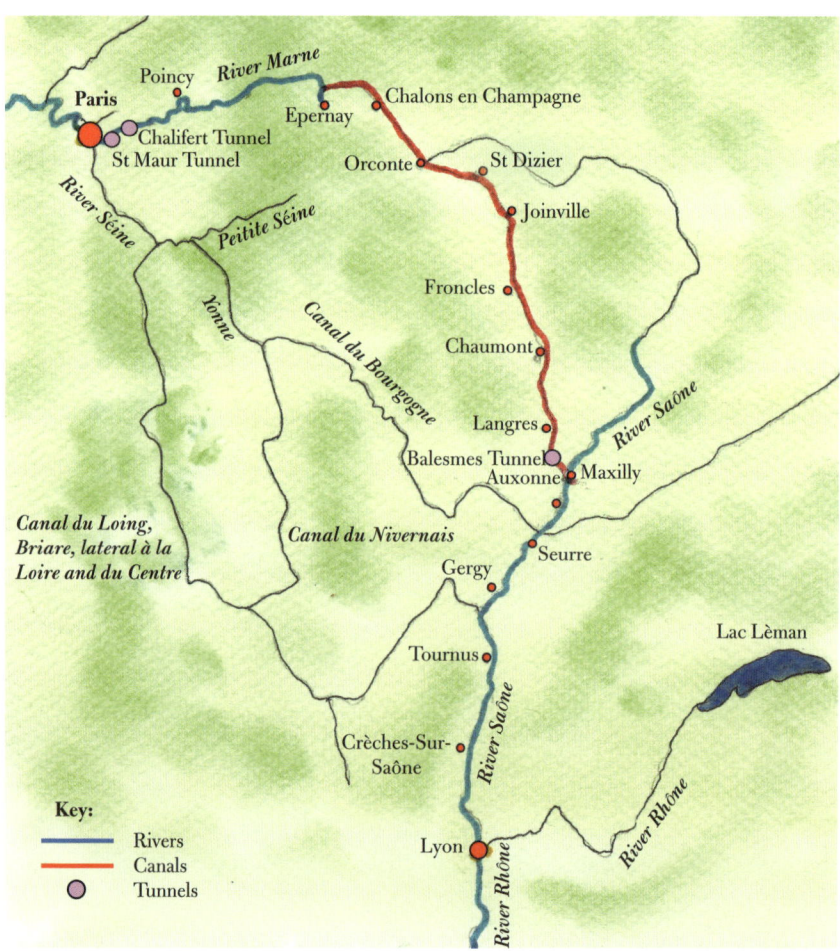

↟ *Paris to River Saône*

➜ *Approach to the St Maur Tunnel*

The Chalifert Tunnel, although shorter than the Saint-Maur, was more challenging. *Écluse No14* Chalifert was manned by the only unhelpful *éclusier* we'd met. He chatted on his mobile phone with his back to us as we mastered a new type of lock, one with a pole to tie up to instead of bollards, then he opened the sluices to full spate before we were ready. Poor little *Barberry* was thrown around like a little old granny on a bouncy castle, her deck cleats groaning under the force as she yawed and bucked.

Our Barbican 33 has a long keel with the addition of a swinging centreplate that is raised and lowered by a line and pulley. The line to raise the centreplate passes through a stainless-steel pipe from the keel to the top of the cabin roof which allows the line to be run back to the cockpit. In this lock, the water turbulence was so fierce that water spurted up through the pipe, erupting as a fountain all over the cabin roof, and soaking Fraser as he perched on the side deck, worrying about a cleat being ripped out.

It was soon over, but as we hadn't been able to contact the *éclusier* via the VHF (he was half a boat length from us, but busy with his personal phone call), I left the boat to ask him if it was okay to pass on through the tunnel.

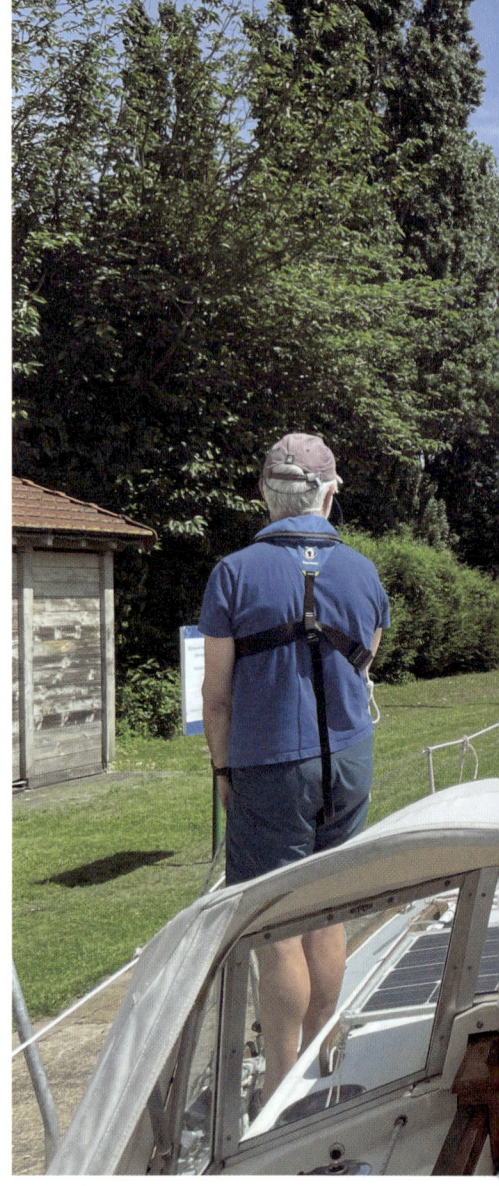

He continued chatting on the mobile, and just waved an arm at me, which I took to mean yes, we could proceed. We were both fairly traumatised by that experience, as we'd just begun to think we were coping quite well with locks. Luckily all the other *éclusiers* have

↟ *Chalifert Lock. Note the red traffic light: this turns green once the upstream gates are fully open.*

been great, keeping an eye on us as they gently open the sluices, and keeping the flow under control.

That first day after leaving Paris, we managed 7 locks, 2 tunnels, and covered 31nm. When we pulled into the tiny little backwater marina at Poincy for the night, the manager appeared impressed. He said it took most people at least two days to reach him from Paris.

That's when we realised since we set off, we'd been racing against deadlines: tidal gates, adverse

↟ *Turbulence as the water enters the lock when rising*

weather forecasts, etc had left us with a habit of rushing. It took some effort to take a deep breath and slow down. Although still anxious about the water levels in the reaches ahead of us, we needed to remember why we were doing this in the first place. We'd longed for the slower pace of life of the inland waterways, and now the forests and meadows were rushing past us in a blur.

The next day, although we covered roughly the same distance, we faced fewer locks and weren't as tired by the time we tied up by the lock at Charly. It was a relief to be away from the noise and commotion of Paris, with its sirens and blasting car horns. Gradually, the French countryside was beginning to work its magic on us.

After Charly, we truly began to embrace the canal life, stopping

Fishermen

Just when you think you're in the middle of nowhere, you catch a glimpse of silver thread, like fine spider silk in the sunlight filtering through the trees. That's all the warning you get for the long rods and lines that can stretch across the entire width of the canal. Usually, they hear us coming and pull the rod in enough for us to pass, but sometimes they're asleep, or maybe off having a wee, because a few times we've had to go to neutral as we drift over a line, hoping we're not going to end up towing a startled *pêcheur* along behind us.

for lunch breaks and finishing the day early. By then, temperatures were rising into the upper 20s and low 30s (Celsius), so we'd gradually moved from long trousers and fleeces to shorts and T-shirts. Birdsong came from every tree, fish leapt with a splash, and we even saw an occasional snake swimming across the canal. We'd also seen every type of freshwater fish imaginable, from carp to catfish.

Back to the locks again. If I seem obsessed with them, it's because they ruled our lives on the waterways. If the locks went smoothly, we covered plenty of ground and could stop early, before the heat of the day made it impossible to continue; if they broke down (which they did with alarming regularity) and we had to wait for a VNF employee to appear

in a little white van, it could slow us down by up to an hour per lock.

By this time, we were past the manned locks and had been handed a *télécommande* (the remote control that would open the locks in the next section) by a friendly *éclusier*. The lock traffic lights were almost always red as we approached, but before we could see the lock, there would be a sign on the bank telling us to use the remote control. We'd press the button for *amont* (upstream) as we headed uphill. If a green light appeared next to the red, all was good, the lock was aware of our presence and getting ready. That's if you could see the green light, because there always seemed to be a bush in front of it. No green light at all, or the presence of flashing red, usually resulted in a call to the VNF office and a request for someone to repair the lock. That's when my pidgin-French was stretched to its limits.

Except for Sean. Sean was a lovely man with a County Mayo accent who spoke fluent English and couldn't be more helpful. We had some lovely chat about places in Mayo, where I have many cousins, while he organised an engineer to fix our lock. He was, however, a little shy about admitting that he could speak English, and stated firmly that he was French, not Irish.

Assuming we saw the green light, the time it took to pass through depended on where the lock was in its cycle. If another boat had recently passed downstream (the opposite direction to us), the lock took less time to prepare but if the last boat had been going

↟ *These blue and red rods are shorter than usual, and not slimy*
➜ *Underground boat tour in Chalons en Champagne*

⬆ *Escaping from Paris*

the same way as us, the chamber needed to empty again before the gates could open. The sluices caused a lot of turbulence and often washed weed and debris out with the water. Eventually the gates would begin to creak open, and we'd start to motor forwards, not entering until we had just a green light, no red.

Once inside the lock, we'd secure *Barberry* by passing fore and aft lines over bollards, which could be at full reach for Fraser even when he stood on the cabin roof with the extra-long boathook. I'd take the aft line and he'd take the forward one, then he would raise the blue control rod a few inches to trigger the filling cycle.

These rods were often covered in slime and weeds and were heavy to lift (I couldn't manage it). The bollards weren't always in the same place for each lock, and the operating rods could be on either side, so we'd go in with long lines on all four quarters just in case. At the last lock in that section, before Épernay, we handed back the *télécommande* and had to learn a new technique.

We had graduated to locks with a turning rod to trigger them. At about the distance from the lock where we would have pressed the button on the remote control,

a piece of tubing dangled from a wire support above the canal. Some of these were long, hanging down almost to the water, and some were short, requiring a bit of a reach. The aim was to approach slowly, then rotate the tube to trigger the lock. We asked the *eclusier* who collected our *télécommande* which way it should be turned. He shrugged and mimed trying both ways to see which worked.

By this time, my boat handling skills had improved to expert level, so I was able to place the boat right next to the pole then stop so Fraser could twist it first one way then the other. The usual traffic light system would tell us when it was safe to enter the lock, and then we'd be back to the blue poles again.

For miles along this stretch, we'd passed hillsides covered in neat rows of grapevines stretching as far as the eye could see. It would have been churlish not to take a small detour into Épernay for a spot of champagne tasting and a tour of the cold cellars lined with ancient stone and brick where the champagne is created and bottled.

After Épernay, we headed to Chalôns-en-Champagne where we found excellent showers, friendly people and, best of all, a huge choice of superb eating places, our favourite of which was the Brasserie St Alp. We also cycled around the town, glad once again of our trusty folding bikes, and even went on a tourist boat tour beneath ancient Chalôns.

At Vitry-le-François, the first lock on the Canal entre Champagne et Bourgogne, we had to collect another new *télécommande*, after we'd risen up in the lock, before the gates would open to let us out. As the height of the water in the lock made it challenging for me to get on and off the boat, Fraser volunteered to go ashore to fetch it. The remote controls were dispensed from a shiny stainless-steel machine on the wall, with clear instructions in French, German and English. Fraser might have managed fine if there hadn't been a friendly Frenchman on the opposite bank, shouting out instructions (in French).

When no *télécommande* emerged from the slot, Fraser reluctantly pressed the intercom button and was met by a splurge of colloquial French. Bear in mind that all his French speaking experience came from a short series of classes in beginner's French he took just before we left, which is why he usually left all the French speaking to me (come to think of it he left

most of the English speaking to me too). Somehow, he managed to answer all the questions (I'm still not certain the answers he gave matched the questions but never mind). In theory, a remote control should then have popped out of the shiny box, but it didn't happen.

After half an hour's frustration, I managed to climb down from the boat and tried my luck with the intercom. The man on the other end told me there was a problem (*quelle surprise*) and that someone was coming to fix it, but he didn't know how long they'd be because they had to drive 30km to us.

Finally, after almost two hours of waiting, a VNF man turned up in his little white van, opened the magic shiny box with a key and handed us the precious remote control that was inside it.

After that, we met the same man several times when he fixed broken locks for us, always giving us a cheery wave as we passed through. I got quite fond of the sight of his white van with its puff of white dust blooming up behind it as it sped along the towpath.

Some of the locks we faced began to be a bit of a stretch for Fraser even with his long boat hook, so we decided to trial a new technique. At one of the locks, I put him ashore with his folding bike and a boat hook (Sir Lancelot on a Brompton) so he cycled ahead to catch my lines as I motored into the locks and handed them up to him.

It worked well, and our Bluetooth headsets earned their keep, allowing us to stay in contact as he told me which side of the lock to go to, and if there was another boat ahead of me.

We'd often see the same boats time and again, leapfrogging each other as we chose different places for lunch stops or overnight stays. It was great to see the familiar blunt bow of a Dutch barge, or the square profile of an electric barge, or the familiar battering ram of the mast on top of a German yacht as we rounded a bend. Everyone seemed to be enjoying the experience as much as us, and we all helped each other out.

⬇ Barberry *almost in the shade in Orconte*

We made a rural stop near the village of Orconte. The guides had promised us a bakery and a pizza restaurant, but the village was dead, just dusty streets with no trace of human presence – apparently many village businesses had closed down since the Covid pandemic. However, Fraser did discover an automatic pizza dispenser that looked a bit like a colourful ATM. It was either that or corned beef hash with tinned veg (again), so I downloaded the app and ordered us both pizzas, with very low expectation of success. Fraser trudged back into the silent, dusty village and returned with two of the most delicious pizzas we've ever tasted. You live and learn!

After Orconte, we spent a noisy night in St Dizier, where the local canal-side bar was hosting a live music event that continued almost until dawn. It might have been more enjoyable if the music had been good, but it sounded like your least favourite uncle singing karaoke at a family wedding after too many shots.

I'd insisted on flying the WOB (Women on Barges) burgee from our radar arch, and as we travelled through France, it had provided us with a ready-made network of fellow boaters as other women waved and pointed to their own WOB burgee. On this occasion, it brought about a new friendship. As we passed a moored boat just before Joinville an excited voice started shouting my name.

Fellow WOB, Helen, had read about our adventures and recognised *Barberry* from her picture. Helen, her husband Steve, and their dog, Daisy moored their beautiful steel cruiser, *Oya*, behind us, beneath the shade of tall trees at Joinville, then we giggled our way through an excellent meal at the hotel there. During the meal, Helen and Steve explained that the extra button on our *télécommande* operates the lock from inside, so we had never needed to use the slippery blue poles after all!

In Joinville, we discovered the frog chorus. Initially, we thought the noise was caused by a problem with the engine but soon realised that it emanated from the canal bank. Hidden in the reeds was an army of amphibians, busily rehearsing for the froggy equivalent of Last Night of the Proms. If we

➜ *Pizza dispenser in Orconte*

Pizzas Fraîches & Artisanales
Pâte Maison

ARTISAN PIZZAÏOLO
PizzaO
Box
ORCONTE

CONSEIL DE CUISSON
Pour les pizzas froides.

🌡️ 220°C

⏱️ 3-4 minutes

Dans un four préchauffé, placez votre pizza sans le disque, sur une grille à mi-hauteur. Bon appétit !

Tapez votre code de Carte Bancaire

Insérez votre monnaie

Comment ça marche ?
① Je choisis mes pizzas
② Je valide mon panier
③ Je procède au paiement
④ Je récupère mes pizzas

Insérez vos billets

TOUCHEZ L'ÉCRAN
POUR COMMENCER

Commandez facilement depuis chez vous !

Téléchargez l'application Smart Pizza

Insérez votre Carte Bancaire

Récupérez votre ticket

Veuillez prendre votre monnaie

Carte Bancaire sans contact

PÂTE FAITE MAISON

📷 Machine sous surveillance

ASSISTANCE PIZZAO
06 31 77 83 50

① **Commandez**
1, 2, 3... PIZZAS

② **Patientez**
1, 2, 3... MINUTES

③ **Dégustez**
1, 2, 3... PIZZAS

FÉDÉRATION
PIZZAIOLOS DE FRANCE

ARTISAN PIZZAÏOLO
PizzaO
Box
24H/24   7J/7

))) **CHAUDE** 3 min

❄️ **FROIDE** 30 sec

TÉLÉCHARGEZ L'APPLICATION & COMMANDEZ VOS PIZZAS

Smart Pizza

stayed totally still, they'd eventually settle down, but if one of us turned over in bed, off they went again at full volume. I began to wonder if this was what had first driven the French to eat *grenouille*, although it might have made more sense to start with the head end, just to shut them up.

We found some wonderful places to stop and top up our supplies as we rose slowly through lock after lock, but gradually we approached the Langres Plateau, where the Canal entre Champagne et Bourgogne passes through the Balesmes Tunnel for almost 5km before descending towards the River Saône. In between the town of Langres and the Saône lies a 74km stretch of canal known as the Green Desert, so named because overnight stopping places are few and far between, and there are no shops or places to buy fuel.

We stocked up so thoroughly in Langres (a long uphill bike ride to the supermarket followed by a terrifying, out-of-control descent with heavy backpacks to the canal) that we were still eating those stores when we reached Greece.

As we approached the tunnel our ears were assaulted by birds screaming, almost deafening. I ducked down as we churned into the darkness, expecting to be attacked at any moment as if we were in an Alfred Hitchcock film, but it turned out it was just a bird scarer, discouraging pigeons from nesting in the tunnel.

For the first kilometre or so there was no lighting in the tunnel, and we relied on Fraser's powerful handheld spotlight, but as we passed a CCTV camera on the wall (I waved at it), the lights magically came on along the full length. I had visions of Sean, the Irish VNF man, nodding off in his chair and not noticing us entering the tunnel, then panicking and hitting the light switch. We got to meet Sean at the next lock, our first down-lock after the long climb, and he looked exactly as I expected: skinny, pale and dressed all in black, even his hat.

The Green Desert lived up to its name. Stopping places were fewer and more isolated than before, with no village boulangeries within easy walking distance, no supermarkets, no fuel. We made it through in three days and finally tied up at Maxilly on 6th June beneath an unrelentingly hot sun. After that, there was only one lock to pass through on the canal before we turned onto the River Saône.

This was also when we heard from Helen and Steve, who we'd

left behind in Joinville, that the VNF were beginning to restrict access to reaches, grouping boats in batches for the locks to save water. We might have been the last boat to pass through unhindered that season.

I tried not to keep reminding Fraser that we were only lucky now because I'd insisted on leaving Ireland in April, knowing this might happen, but I think he could tell from my smirks whenever we heard about water shortages on the canals.

♠ *Bullfrog chorus in Joinville*

Going down the locks was far easier than going up, as we could see the bollards on approach, and only needed to drop a middle line over one of them to secure the boat. There's little turbulence travelling in this direction, so less stress about fenders popping out, and no one needs to balance on the coach roof with an extra-long boat hook. Fraser even let me take the lines once or twice, while he steered the boat into the lock.

Lessons Learned

- Information from other waterways users is invaluable. It saved us from being turned back along our original route and made it possible for us to pass unhindered through the canals of France.

- Locks rule your life on the canals. A good day is one where only one lock breaks down, and the VNF engineer is only a few kilometres away.

- Each lock is different, so you can't afford to grow complacent.

- Down locks are far easier than up locks.

- Always remember which direction you're going so you press the correct button on the télécommande and don't break the entire system

- If you're going to do this trip in either direction, set off as early in the season as possible (bearing in mind that maintenance mostly happens in the winter, and locks can be closed for major repair work). Not long after us, the CCB (Canal entre Champagne et Bourgogne) was closed to pleasure boats completely due to low water levels.

- The VNF have an excellent website and an app (Navi) through which they announce closures, and you can register for email notifications. It also has a useful route planning function.

- The télécommande can be used to operate locks, saving a struggle with slimy poles.

14

THE SAÔNE AND RHÔNE

The River Saône was kind to us. The canals were an amazing experience, and locks that wouldn't behave, or long waits for engineers were all a part of the adventure, as we cruised so close to nature (sometimes pulling it out of our water intake), yet when the banks receded, and we moved onto a deep river meandering through fields and small towns, it felt as if we'd entered another country.

Our first stop on the Saône was at Auxonne, a truly beautiful French town with ancient buildings, great restaurants, and friendly people. We spent two nights there, enjoying cycling around the historical walled town, and sipping beer in street cafés, but we needed to keep moving south, as our mast was due to be delivered to Port Napoléon on 30 June.

Between Auxonne and Seurre, we were delayed by a rescue mission. We came across a small hire boat half-hidden in the bushes at the side of the river not long after we'd left Auxonne.

'They're probably having an early lunch,' said Fraser, who didn't want to stop so soon after leaving (I'd dragged him out before breakfast to make headway in the cool of the early morning). 'If they needed help, they'd be waving their arms.'

Hire boats do some odd stuff, but when one of the crew started waving both arms in the international sign for distress, even Fraser had to agree that we needed to investigate.

I reduced throttle and turned *Barberry* towards the bank, which looked horribly shallow, and booby trapped by the stiff limbs of half-submerged trees. I nosed the boat cautiously into the shallows, bow-first to protect our propeller and rudder from damage.

The plan was to try to throw a line to them so we could reverse towards deeper water, dragging them with us. Her crew of three very

✦ *Fraser pulling weed out of the water intake*

tired-looking people were delighted to see us as they caught the line Fraser passed, making it fast on a bow cleat. *Barberry's* Beta 35HP engine had no difficulty hauling out the smaller boat, and once clear of vegetation we managed to pull the other boat alongside and secure her fore and aft for a side tow.

Apparently, this Greek family had lost engine propulsion in the hire boat the night before and had been drifted into the trees by the wash from several passing boats, none of which had slowed to help them. The hire company (which shall remain nameless) hadn't answered the phone until morning and had said they could only come out to help if the family could get the boat to a jetty close to a road.

We'd passed a small, shallow jetty (not suitable for *Barberry*) a few kilometres upstream. This was back the way we'd come, which put Fraser in an even more grumpy mood, but we managed to build up a bit of momentum before releasing the disabled boat to drift over to the jetty, where they tied themselves up. Eventually a van appeared on the road, and a man in overalls got out.

On hearing that we were bound for the Ionian, the grateful

➜ *Rivers Saône and Rhône*

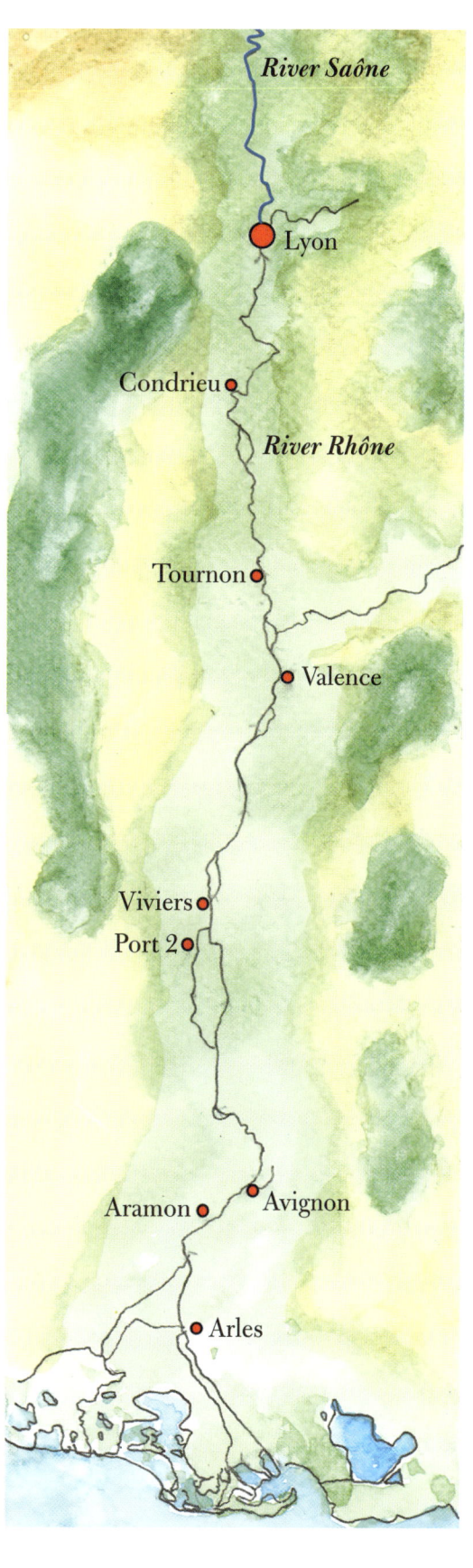

holiday makers had offered us free accommodation in their apartment once we reached Greece. Sadly, not only did we fail to get their contact details, but we were also too busy with the rescue to remember to reach for a camera, so we didn't get a single photo of them either.

As if our day hadn't been strange enough, we encountered a police/military exercise a little further downstream. A police launch approached us at high speed (I was grumbling about inconsiderate river users until I saw the markings) and ordered us to stay where we were until further notice.

It turned out they were dropping men into the river from a helicopter, then retrieving them again and again. A bit like dunking biscuits in tea and hoping you don't lose any.

Seurre was our next stop, a beautiful town with friendly staff in the tourism office who even kept the *capitainerie* open an extra half hour in the evening for us, so we could get our freshly washed bedding dried in the tumble dryer.

Our Brompton folding bikes allowed us to cycle out of town to a lovely little folk museum with ancient buildings, salvaged and rebuilt to give a taste of life in the region over the centuries. We seemed to be the only visitors that weekend.

By this time, we were beginning to appreciate the full force of the southern climate. The temperatures climbed dramatically as we wended our way south until by late morning, even with a parasol up, we were beginning to melt. This is when we began setting our alarms for early starts to try to get some miles under our belts before the full heat of the day, ending our journeys around lunchtime so we could crash out in the cabin with all hatches open and a fan on.

Of course, this often led to missed breakfasts and delayed lunches, which made Fraser restless. Apparently, fruit and biscuits on the move are no substitute for a leisurely lunch at a proper table with plates and cutlery.

In this way, we passed through Gergy, which was a free stop with a restaurant and a village a short walk away. It was on the restaurant menu that we first encountered *grenouille*, so maybe this is where the frog chorus from Joinville ended up.

Tournus came next, a breathtakingly beautiful town with narrow streets, ancient buildings,

← *Cycling through an ancient archway in Auxonne*

↟ *Dunking French soldiers for some reason*

and not too expensive at €8 for a 33ft boat on the pontoon (including water and electric); then Crêches-sur-Saône, which both our out-of-date *Fluviacarte* and the Cruising Association's wonderful guide to the French inland waterways promised us would be a perfect stopover.

According to the guides, this *halte* offered showers, a laundry, and even a swimming area. With this in mind, we rushed along in the hope of finding a space on the pontoon before hordes of hire boats descended. We were pleasantly surprised to find an empty pontoon with water and electric points, so we tied up, had lunch, then went up to the restaurant for beer and ice cream (I'm not usually a beer drinker, but there's something irresistible about condensation

↓ *The halte at Gergy with Barberry tucked into a tiny space at the end*

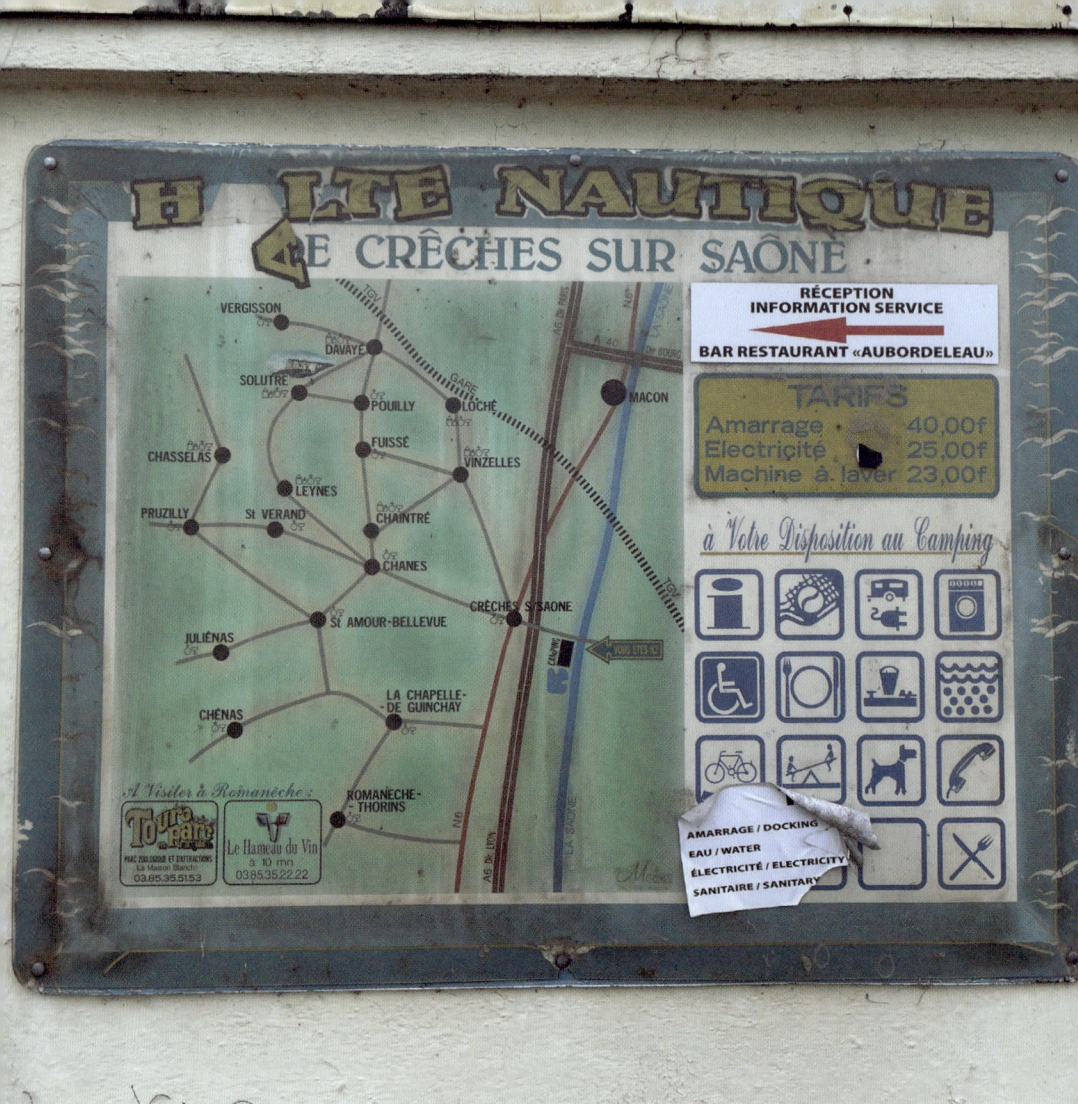

↟ *Sign at Crêches-sur-Saône. Note tariffs are in Francs so this sign dates back to before 2002*

running down the outside of a glass brimming with golden lager on a baking hot day). The restaurant owner told us that there were indeed showers at the campsite just behind us and that berthing here was now free of charge, including water and electric.

We headed off to investigate, shower bags and towels in hand, but as soon as we entered the site, we were accosted by an irate manager. The campsite, she informed us, was no longer municipal but private, and she certainly didn't want any smelly boat bums messing it up (or words to that effect – my French isn't that strong).

Tails between our legs, we scuttled back to the boat for a shower instead and later returned to the restaurant for dinner. When we told the owner that sailors were no longer welcome at the campsite, he didn't seem totally surprised which made us wonder if we'd been pawns in a feud between him and the campsite.

Barberry may be a small boat, but she is equipped with a shower of sorts. Her heads compartment is pint-sized, and the hottest space in the boat, so a weak, trickly boat shower is never really refreshing. Before the shower, we have to remove all towels, loo roll etc from the heads so they don't get wet; after the shower we have to mop up the floors and pump the bilges, by which time we're usually even sweatier than when we started.

⚓ Barberry *on a tiny pontoon just north of Lyon*

It seemed ironic that in Northern Ireland, when we had wind for sailing (and a mast), we rarely ran the engine, so we had no hot water for showers that might have helped us defrost our frozen bodies; in the inland waterways we ran the engine for several hours a day, generating gallons of hot water, yet all we yearned for was a cool shower.

The next obvious stopping place would have been Lyon, France's second largest city after Paris, but the pilot books weren't optimistic. Although there are numerous free

quays to tie up to, there were also dark hints of theft and vandalism, including locals cutting lines of moored boats. There is one secure marina in Lyon, but when we researched it, it turned out to be closed for that season. Instead, we spent a peaceful night just north of the city on a tiny rural pontoon with no facilities. We ate breakfast in the cockpit the following morning while scullers and racing eights rowed past us.

Lyon did look beautiful from the water, boasting some magnificent buildings, but it was also marred

↓ *Typical waiting pontoon*

⚓ *The beauty and elegance of Lyon was marred by graffiti*

by graffiti on almost every wall we passed. We didn't feel much regret at missing it.

Immediately after Lyon, the River Saône joins the mighty River Rhône, where we encountered our first really deep lock, Pierre Bénite, at 11.8m depth. This was where I always began to get a little twitchy, it's hard enough chatting on the VHF in your own language but chatting with someone who speaks rapid and colloquial French adds a whole new dimension to the challenge.

Speaking was fine, because I'd had time to think about what I was going to say: 'This is the *plaisancier*, *Barberry*, heading downstream towards your lock. We hope to be with you in around 15 minutes. Please may we enter the lock?' I had a rough idea of what the reply might be, but reality never tied in with expectation. Even when I asked a yes-or-no-answer style question, I still got a spiel of incomprehensible French in reply. Phoning them rather than using the VHF was easier, but still challenging.

After floundering in a morass of Franglais (me) and impatient French (the *éclusier*), I usually ended up saying, meekly, 'We'll just wait for the green light, shall we?'

These bigger locks on the Rhône have waiting pontoons for *plaisanciers* (pleasure boats) as well as rows of giant dolphins (big pillars that stick up out of the water and allow a barge to go alongside) for commercial vessels.

If there was a red traffic light when we arrived, we would always try to tie up to the pontoon because it usually meant there was a boat about to enter from the other direction, so it would take a while; if it was showing red and green, that meant they were preparing the lock, which could take up to 20+ minutes for the deep ones, so we'd often just hover near the pontoon, keeping a wary eye out

⚓ *Hotel barge emerging from Sablons lock*

behind for any *péniches* or hotel barges approaching as they always have priority.

Once all boats were securely moored inside the lock, and the *éclusier* was satisfied that everyone had remembered their lifejackets, the gates closed and the lock began to fill. These big locks have floating bollards in the walls which make tying up far easier, but as the water level drops, the screech of metal on metal can make a cacophony. Once the water level had fallen to match that of the lower river, the downstream gates began to open. These vary, but on the huge locks of the Rhône they are often lifting barriers that rise up majestically, river water cascading from the metal. As we didn't have a bimini, we usually got quite wet as we passed beneath.

The Rhône's currents were far less ferocious than we'd expected, largely due to the dry weather. It felt as if we were the only boat heading south, but we did pass several yachts with masts mounted along their decks going in the opposite direction. We were a little worried in case they didn't get through, because by then we'd heard of closures due to low water behind us.

Our first stop after Lyon was at Les Roches de Condrieu, a nice little marina with good facilities. Our payment for the berth came with free passes for a nearby swimming lake, which we made good use of. We stayed in the cool water until we looked like a pair of prunes, then rehydrated with a cold beer at the bar before cycling (somewhat wobbly by then) back to the boat.

After that came Valence. By then we needed fuel, and the guidebooks assured us that there'd be fuel on offer seven days a week at Valence. There wasn't. The pumps were locked up and there was no one in the *capitainerie*. The next day, when we asked why, the man behind the counter gave an expressive shrug. Apparently he had no more idea than us why his staff member hadn't turned up, but we did manage to get fuel there that day before leaving.

We didn't hang around too long on the Rhône. Viviers was beautiful but mostly memorable for the Portakabin shower that was like a steam room, and for the mountain of whitebait Fraser accidentally

ordered, thinking he'd ordered a fish supper (the menu called it fish and chips).

The tail-end of the journey that we'd estimated would take four days only took two, not least because of a dearth of good stopping places. We had intended to overnight in a place called Port 2 (odd sort of name, but it was listed in all the river guides and had good reviews). This meant backtracking a few miles up a spur of the Rhône, but the promise of water, electric, showers and even a laundry lured us up there.

As soon as we made the turn into the side-branch, the entire nature of the river changed. The banks closed in, with lush greenery overhanging the water and both insect and bird sounds we hadn't heard before, like something from a jungle. A couple of sinister-looking French military landing craft were sitting in the shadows along the bank, complete with armed crews and machine guns mounted on the bows. We gave them a cheery wave and continued on, slogging against a fairly strong current. The old 'Irish tourists abroad act' usually does the trick.

On our left, an eerie ruined building came into view, covered in creepers and vines. It looked as if someone had tried to build a hotel but given up partway. We felt as if we might catch a glimpse of Sly Stallone, complete with bandana and blood-stained vest, dodging between the trees with his machine gun.

Finally, we spotted a bright blue construction up ahead and our spirits lifted, but as we drew closer something didn't look quite right. Where were all the boats? We passed a couple of half-sunken wrecks, then a fisherman on the bank, who glared at us and didn't return our wave. The birdsong had ceased, leaving only insect noises.

We went on, because we were exhausted and desperate for somewhere safe to tie up for the night, but it quickly became clear that Port 2 was not suitable. The skeleton of walkways was still there, a couple of listing hulks alongside, paint peeling and lines mired with slime. More half-sunken boats lay near the entrance. We seriously considered going inside, but all the finger pontoons had been removed, the *capitainerie* was

◄ The ancient town of Viviers

clearly abandoned with its door swinging open on squealing hinges, and bits of twisted metal hung from the walkways. Ropes stretched out across the entrance, disappearing beneath the water, a hazard to the propeller.

I quietly backed the boat out again the way we'd gone in, then opened the throttle to escape downstream as fast as we could.

However tired we were, anything was better than staying there.

Aramon, our next planned stopping place, was another 4–5 hours downstream, beyond Avignon, so we phoned ahead and asked if they could take us. Luckily, they had a space. We were grateful for *Barberry's* 1.2m draught as we nudged inside a pontoon marked as shallow and

↓ *The remains of Port 2 Marina*

tied up in a perfect *Barberry*-sized gap amongst small motorboats.

A friendly one-legged man caught our lines and helped us tie up, chattering away in rapid French that we were too tired to follow. He unfastened Fraser's spring line then retied it as a short midships line for some reason. Once he'd wandered off, we noticed all the other boats were tied up the same way, snatching badly every time a passing *péniche* sent wash into the bank. We sneakily retied the spring once he'd gone, and *Barberry's* motion improved.

The next day, we set off early again to take advantage of the slightly cooler temperatures. We'd have liked to have stopped in Arles, to see the famous Roman amphitheatre, but none of the river

↑ *La Péniche restaurant barge in Arles*

guides were optimistic about our chances. Apparently, you could raft alongside *La Péniche*, a restaurant barge, but when we reached it we found a tiny, scruffy speedboat tied up to the ladder. It looked as if it had been there for years, and the whole barge looked derelict with peeling paint and green slime along the waterline.

So we continued onwards towards the beckoning sea. Making good time on the lower Rhône, we reached the lock into Port St Louis du Rhône around 1400 and radioed the *éclusier* to let him know we were there. The lock and lifting bridge openings run to a schedule which is published in the river guides, but there's always a chance that they'll let a pleasure boat through along with a commercial barge if you're in the right place at the right time and speak sweetly to the lock keeper. As the next scheduled opening in

↓ *Waiting for the lock and lifting bridge at Port St Louis du Rhône*

↑ *Excited as we sit in the lock waiting for the lifting bridge*

our direction wasn't for another couple of hours, we were hoping for the best.

As we sat there, munching a late lunch of fruit and bread, we spotted a familiar face cycling past. It was Stu, from the YouTube channel *Sailing Seabird*. He came over for a brief chat and we arranged to meet him and his partner, Marina, another day.

We must have spoken sweetly enough to the *éclusier*, because we'd barely tied up to the wall (beneath the 'no mooring' sign, as that was the only place with bollards) when he radioed us to say that we could go through along with a giant barge.

After all the enormous locks we'd already negotiated, this one was a slight let down. We travelled up about 10cm! It wasn't far after that to pass through the port, out to sea, and then back along a marked channel into the marina at Port Napoléon where we planned to meet our mast.

As we passed beneath the lifting bridge, into the basin at Port St Louis du Rhône, a huge rush of relief came over both of us. We'd done it. The battles against tidal overfalls down the east coast of Ireland, the washing machine of the Bristol Channel, all the various rivers and canals of France, and we'd finally reached the shining, blue waters of the Mediterranean. We were ahead of schedule by almost a week as our mast wasn't due to arrive until 30 June, but we didn't care.

Port Napoléon is a good place to stay, either in transit like us, or to base a boat for cruising. There are great showers, a lovely restaurant, every type of boat repair specialist on site, well-stocked chandlery and helpful *capitainerie* staff. There's also a lovely beach a 20-minute cycle away but you have to be careful not to get distracted by flocks of flamingos searching for food in the brackish waters.

In the town of Port St Louis du Rhône, about 15 minutes away by bike, there's a good supermarket and plenty of eating places all around. Depending on which route you take, you might also see some of the famous white horses of the Camargue. The tourist office (in an ancient stone tower) is worth a visit too. Tell them you live on a boat in the marina, and they'll let you browse the upper floors for free as a resident. Sadly, the only black Camargue bull we saw during our stay was in the form of a trophy head on the wall of the tourist office.

We spent about ten days in Port Napoléon, reprovisioning, swimming, testing out the restaurant and chandlers, more swimming, and chatting with Stuart and Marina from *Sailing Seabird*. They're worth watching, if you haven't discovered them so far. They bought an abandoned (waterlogged) Gulfstar 41 from the yard in Port Napoléon for €1 and are in the process of restoring her to her former glory. Such a motivated couple, an absolute lesson in determination, hard work, and can-do attitude. It was an inspiration to spend time with the pair of them.

One huge disadvantage of the Camargue is the biting insects. One of my cousins, who knows the area well, told me Camargue mosquitoes can bite through jeans, and I believe her. I'm always a mosquito magnet,

Port St Louis du Rhône

Port Navy Service

Port Napoléon

Camargue
National Park

⚓ *Route from Rhône to Port Napoléon showing road to beach*

Key:

- 🟣 Lock from Rhône to sea
- 🟡 Lifting Bridge
- 🟢 Site of sunken ketch on sandbank
- ▬ Roads

Beach

but even Fraser complained this time when he too got bitten.

One touristy trip we'd promised ourselves was to take the bus back to Arles. It's about an hour each way, the bus is air conditioned, and you can usually bring bikes in the luggage compartment if you ask nicely. We bought a multi-attraction ticket that allowed us into the Roman amphitheatre, the Roman theatre, the old Roman baths, and the underground *Cryptoporticus,*

an underground storage and administrative complex that dates back to the first century BCE, which was blessedly cool.

At last our mast arrived, a day ahead of schedule, and was placed on rolling stands by the efficient yard staff. Fraser and I spent a sweaty afternoon removing all the padding that had kept it safe in transit then began preparing it to be fitted again. The sun was baking hot, and dust clouds rose

↟ *Folding bikes at the bus stop in Port St Louis*
➜ Cryptoporticus *beneath the streets of Arles*

⚓ *Unwrapping* Barberry's mast

around our feet as we walked, a huge contrast to when we wrapped it for transport in Rouen six weeks earlier in pouring rain. We told the yard that we were ready to go a day early if there was an available slot, and they said they'd see what they could do. Up to that point, their crane had been out of action, but

luckily, they had it fixed by the time our mast arrived.

Early the next morning, we were woken by someone knocking on the boat. The yard staff said they could put *Barberry's* mast on in the next hour or so if we could be ready in time. We were out of bed and scrambling into clothes before they'd finished speaking. *Barberry* had spent long enough as a river boat; it was time to restore her to her true function again, and we couldn't wait.

Fraser had spent some time replacing the masthead fittings the previous day, including the wind indicator and the LED tri-light/ anchor light combo. There was no indication on the light fitting as to which way it should point, and with LEDs, you can't see the colours unless it's switched on, so we had to search online for the answer.

That morning, there was a panicky rotation to the correct orientation before the crane lifted it.

It's always nerve-wracking, watching your precious mast being lifted onto your boat, but the staff were 100% professional, and we had total faith in them. Once it was seated, the men leaned back against the crane with hand rolled ciggies to let Fraser and I attach all the rigging. There was quite a stiff breeze blowing by then, the mistral that this region is famous for, so the port side stays attached

↟ *Port Napoléon's crane and cherry picker*

easily, but the starboard side ones seemed slightly short due to the effects of the wind on boat and mast. The yard staff tried hauling down on the wires, but the only way we managed to get them to reach was by having me dangle like a fat orangutan from the starboard side mast steps, counterbalancing the wind. For once my weight worked to my advantage.

Once all the rigging was secured, a small and disreputable-looking man was sent up in a cherry-picker to replace the wind indicator. We had booked 30 minutes with the crane, and we were away from the dock well before our time was up, much to our surprise – it had seemed to take forever to get those starboard side stays attached. We headed back to our berth and had a celebratory cold fruit juice from the fridge before tensioning the rigging and putting the sails back on.

Now, all we needed was a fair forecast to sail east towards Nice, where we'd arranged to visit family, but this was the Gulf of Lions, named for the ferocity of its dangerous winds, so we knew we might have to wait for a while.

Lessons Learned

- Don't necessarily believe cruising guides on the rivers and canals. Admittedly, our *Fluviacartes* were out of date, but our other sources were not, yet still we were misled.

- There are fewer safe stopping places than you might imagine on the bigger rivers, and we found internet satellite view gave us a good idea of what to expect.

- Never underestimate the effects of heat. Europe has experienced extreme temperatures in recent years, and it really can sap your energy.

- Shade is almost impossible to find on the Saône and Rhône, so any sort of cockpit cover/bimini/parasol is invaluable. It doesn't need to look pretty.

- The flies in the Camargue are vicious: mosquitoes that love to eat vulnerable Irish people. Use fly netting on every opening of your boat, and wear a good insect repellent, especially if going out in the evening.

➔ *Mast back up after nearly two months as a river boat*

PART 4

Remembering how to sail

15

SOUTHERN FRANCE AND CORSICA

After a few days champing at the bit and waiting for the mistral to ease, we spotted a forecast for a westerly wind that would carry us to Nice so we could meet up with my cousin, Monique, and her family. We left Port Napoléon early on the 4th of July, passing the sad evidence of a ketch that ran aground on a sand spit in these tempestuous waters and is gradually being engulfed by the beach. Only her masts now show above the waves, a warning to all of us.

Once out into the gulf, *Barberry* cut through the waves, as happy to be free of brown water and weed as we were. Heavy commercial traffic in the Golfe du Lion kept us on our toes as we tried to remember which lines and sheets to pull, and when (there may have been a crash gybe in the mix somewhere). Tugs and giant tankers criss-crossed the bay, but before too long we left them in our wake and began to enjoy spectacular views of cliffs and tiny *calanques* (deep, narrow bays similar to fjords) with a strip of pale sand at the end of them.

We spent our first night back at sea anchored in the Calanque de Sormiou, which is when Fraser discovered a casting defect in our brand-new windlass which was now leaking oil. It was still working but clearly needed to be sorted. I must give a shout out here to both Marine Superstore, from whom we bought the unit, and to Lofrans,

who replaced the unit speedily and at no cost, shipping it out to Nice for us.

We'd spent years dreaming of crystal clear blue waters with shoals of fish surrounding the boat, so we wasted no time getting into our swimming costumes to check the anchor. I went in first, gasping at the cold shock of deep water (around 11m depth), and quickly decided that the anchor was probably fine. When Fraser saw my reaction, he changed his mind about swimming, so I grabbed the swim ladder to climb up it. Every time I got my feet onto it and tried to pull myself up, the hinged ladder swung beneath the transom and I, being on the heavy side (no longer an advantage), was

A sad sight: a ketch slowly disappearing into the sand

↟ *Calanque de Sormiou and our first taste of crowded Mediterranean anchorages*

unable to lift my entire sodden bodyweight with my arms. We'd never tried the ladder before, because you'd be crazy to swim from the boat in Northern Ireland.

'I'll swim to the beach,' I said cheerily, trying not to let my teeth chatter. 'You can pick me up with the dinghy.'

I'm too fat and unfit to climb into the dinghy from the water, in case you're wondering why I didn't use it to get out, but I soon realised the beach was a long way away, and there was a brisk offshore breeze.

Quick change of plan. I headed for the nearby cliffs, where a tempting ledge offered a platform from which to climb into the dinghy. Only when I got closer did I appreciate how jagged the local rock formations were. Still, I climbed onto a partially submerged shelf and waited for my Sir Lancelot to save me.

He was quite grouchy by the time he'd rowed over. I tried to coax him closer with endearments such as, 'Get that blasted boat over here and stop whining,' but he stayed tantalisingly out of reach, muttering about punctured dinghies being no help to anyone.

Eventually, he was washed within reach by an errant wave, and I managed to grab the dinghy before he had a chance to escape. If you've ever seen a walrus wallowing onto a rock, you'll have a fair idea of how graceful and elegant I was as I entered the dinghy, soaking Fraser as I flopped into the bottom of the boat.

Once I was safely aboard *Barberry*, I reminded Fraser that the anchor remained unchecked. He'd got quite sweaty with the rowing, so he didn't put up too much of a fight. Once he'd dived down and reassured himself that the old CQR was well bedded in, he headed back to the boat.

'While you're down there, maybe you should free up the paddle wheel?' I suggested (it had become clogged with weed early on in France). I'm not sure what he replied as it was muffled by the snorkel. Still, he managed to free it up, so we had boat speed once more.

The next day brought us to another anchorage in the Baie du Gau, a trip of between 9 and 10 hours that took us past the Île

↟ *A calm morning in the anchorage at Baie du Gau*

de Porquerolles, a very popular beauty spot. With 20–25 knots behind her, *Barberry* really lifted her skirts and flew along. Dreaming of moments like these had kept us going through all the dark years while wind and rain hammered at the windows in County Down, and now it was coming true.

The autopilot came under a fair bit of strain that day, and began to make a loud clunking sound every so often. We disengaged it and hand steered most of the way, as we felt we were better at anticipating waves than a computer. The wind continued to pick up and by the time we reached our chosen anchorage, every yacht in the area had also decided it would be a sheltered spot to ride out the wind, so there were at least a score of masts clogging the bay.

↓ *Photos never seem to show just how choppy the conditions are*

We managed to find a patch of sand on which to drop the anchor, to the outside of all the other boats. At least we wouldn't be overlying anyone's anchor chain. Shortly after, several more yachts turned up and anchored outside of us, so we felt a bit less like outliers.

The trusty CQR held, despite it being far too windy and choppy to dive in to check it, and we had a comfortable night with the anchor alarm set. By morning, the mistral had blown itself out and we awoke to flat calm, with a spectacular sunrise.

The last leg to Nice, at over 11 hours the longest hop since leaving the Camargue, took us past St Tropez, Cannes and Antibes, which each turned our chartplotter green with hundreds of AIS targets, mostly superyachts. We set a course and engaged the autopilot,

which still clunked despite the more benign conditions. About an hour into the journey, it gave up completely, so we took turns at hand steering.

Our wonderful friend and Raymarine rep, Brian, texted to say that he'd replace the unit under warranty. As we planned to nip home for a couple of days from Nice to catch up with family and friends, the timing couldn't have been better.

We'd been lucky to book a berth in the old harbour in Nice through the Navily app, thanks to a cancellation, and they kindly let us leave *Barberry* there for 12 days in total while we awaited delivery of our replacement windlass and flew home to collect the new autopilot unit.

The *marinero* who helped us moor up had no idea how nervous we both were. We'd Med-moored in Greece and Turkey on flotilla holidays about 30 years ago, but we'd always been nursed by a lead boat crew. This was our first time solo, and with a long keel lady who has her own views about going astern. I have to admit that our secret weapon, the bow thruster,

→ *First time Med-moored in Nice*

has been a life saver. Without it, tight manoeuvres astern would have been a nightmare, and it was very tight indeed in Nice. When the *marinero* praised us for our efficient boat handling (and he knew I was cheating from the bubbles emerging at the bow), I could have burst with pride.

The marina is right in the heart of the old town, and absolutely beautiful with restaurants, shops, a chandler, and a stony beach just around the corner from the harbour.

We spent a wonderful evening before we left, eating pizzas on the terrace with my cousins. They live in an old farmhouse that clings to the side of a gorge and has spectacular views in all directions. The next morning, we dragged our heavy hold bag the 500m or so to the tram station at the port and headed off for the airport. The bag contained all our winter woollies and the autopilot (nicknamed Robbie, from the film *Forbidden Planet*).

Once home, it was great to spend time with our extended

⚓ *Fraser modifying our swim ladder in Nice*

family, some of whom had flown in from Scotland, but the cold, damp weather reminded us why we'd headed south in the first place. We'd forgotten just how green Ireland is, and how soggy. The tough Scottish cousins joined our tough Northern Irish son in the icy waters of Donaghadee for a swim while we paddled and shivered.

Our son, Patrick, is the only one of the three children still sailing as an adult. He's a very handy crew member and thinks fear is for wimps (we are clearly both wimps). On a whim, he followed us out to Nice on a one-way ticket to try to get some colour onto his pasty Irish skin.

By the time he joined us, Fraser had installed the replacement windlass and the new autopilot, so we were good to go. He also modified the swim ladder by adding a thick block of wood behind it (the remains of one of our trusty fender boards from the canals) so it wouldn't swing inwards as soon as weight was put on it. Even Fraser had found it almost impossible to climb out the way it was, and a fender behind it just wasn't enough.

We enjoyed one more wonderful family evening with my cousins, then set off on the 18-hour sail to Corsica. We reverted to our old watch system, which was a bit of a pull after so many lazy days, but sailing the Mediterranean at night is magical, so it wasn't much of a chore. Patrick volunteered to take a watch, but didn't argue especially hard when we told him he didn't need to.

The clear night sky was scattered with stars, and the boat left a trail of phosphorescence in her wake. Around midnight, several somethings broached alongside the boat, splashing heavily back into the water. I'm guessing dolphins, but everything seems bigger and louder at night, so I'll admit to thinking whales until common sense caught up with me.

We reached our destination, an anchorage at La Revellata near Calvi, at about 0730, dropping anchor in about 7m of sand, carefully avoiding beds of seagrass (*Posidonia spp*), which are protected. We dived in for a swim to freshen up after the long night, then had breakfast in the cockpit. Snorkelling was a joy in these warm, clear waters, right up to the point where I made contact with a small reddish-brown jellyfish, *Pelagia noctiluca*. Boy, do those little guys pack a punch!

Despite a sting that wrapped around my thigh, I was able to

swim back to the boat and even climb the ladder, thanks to Fraser's modifications. Luckily for me (but not for him), my brother-in-law had recently been stung while on holiday in Majorca, and he'd been telling us that vinegar was the best treatment. I use white vinegar to clean the toilet bowl, so Fraser fetched it and sprayed my leg: instant relief.

I blame the jellyfish for what happened next. In my drive to conserve water (because I don't like marinas), I decided to prewash the breakfast bowls in a bucket of seawater before rinsing them in fresh. Obviously, the sting must have affected my brain, because I washed the bowls and the cups, then threw out the dregs into the bay. With the spoons still in it. Three beautiful stainless-steel spoons that were part of a set. The water was so clear that we could see them gleaming in the sunlight on the sand 7.5m below. Patrick offered to dive for them, but I was worried it might be a bit too deep and declined the offer. They're probably still there, if anyone wants to retrieve them.

It turns out that this north-

↓ *Calvi Citadel viewed from our mooring*

western corner of Corsica is a real wind acceleration zone, as we discovered when we tried to go south the next morning. As soon as we cleared the anchorage, we had 20–30 knots on the nose with steep seas to match. We were barely making 1.5–2 knots at full throttle, so we decided to turn back. Too ashamed to reappear in the same anchorage, we went on around the corner to pick up a mooring ball in Calvi Bay where we remained for the next three days as the wind built up to a howling 30+ knots.

Calvi is well worth a visit if you're ever in the area. The Citadel rises in a mound of ancient buildings overlooking the bay, and you can buy delicious home-made ice cream to eat while you take photographs of your boat from above.

There are useful shops a short walk from the marina, and so many excellent restaurants along the seafront that I'd be hard pressed to name a favourite, plus you can leave your tender safely at the steps inside the marina. The wind continued to rise so after a very wet dinghy ride back to the boat with tummies full of pizza, we decided that the water taxi

Lessons Learned

- Never go for a swim from the boat if you're not confident that you can climb back aboard. Check if your swim ladder is fit for purpose.

- You don't realise how much you rely on an autopilot until it's not there. Hand steering in 20–30-knot winds for hours is tiring.

- White vinegar is good for jellyfish stings (and for cleaning boat toilets).

- Cutlery sinks, and stainless steel is not magnetic (we tried).

- When the forecast is for strong headwinds and your boat isn't great to windward, turn over and go back to sleep. There's always another day.

- Canadair pilots are incredible, but Corsica is tinder dry.

was a better option for future trips ashore. Not cheap, but at least you don't get drenched. It picked us up from our boat in 30 knots of wind without fuss.

Our next attempt to head south was more successful. We still had strong headwinds initially, but they gradually eased, and by the time we turned the corner into Ajaccio Bay, it had become a mere light breeze.

Ajaccio is a place we'd have liked to have had more time to explore, but the weather forecast was fair for one more leap south, then it was due to blow a gale again, so we set off at 0700 towards the marina of Pianttoli in Figari Bay.

Figari is a long, thin bay lined with spurs and outcrops of rock that reach towards the buoyed channel as if trying to lure sailors towards them. A sunken sailboat lay as a warning not to stray too far from the channel, or to get distracted by the golden beaches and historical towers on the way in.

We spent four nights at Figari and were relieved to be tucked away safely as the winds gusted to 40–50 knots. A RIB a few berths down from us broke free during the windiest night and was left dangling by her slime line (aka lazy line, which most marinas now seem to have installed in lieu of anchoring).

There are no shops near the marina, but there is an arrangement with the local supermarket, who send a car and driver to collect hungry sailors, then return them to the marina with all their shopping. Patrick's bottomless pit of a stomach had hit our stores hard.

One afternoon we were having a

siesta in the relative cool of the cabin when a plane flew low overhead. This wasn't unusual as there was an airport nearby, but this one sounded as if it had almost hit the mast.

We raced up into the cockpit just in time to see a second plane approaching. We all ducked as it passed over us, still descending. It was one of the distinctive yellow and red Canadair fire-fighting planes. When we looked the other way, there was a plume of white smoke from the tinder-dry land a mile or so behind us.

Before long three of these planes were flying a complex pattern, swooping down to pick up water from the shallow bay, then circling around to dump it on the fire. With incredible skill they skimmed the masts in the marina and somehow managed not to take out the kite surfers (and one terrified little sailing boat that bolted for cover) as they filled their tanks with seawater.

Shortly after this, our ever-hungry crew member decided it was time for him to head back to the real world again. We waved at his plane as he flew over us and the next morning we set our bows towards Sardinia.

⚓ *Canadair plane firefighting in Corsica*

16

SARDINIA, SICILY AND THE STRAITS OF MESSINA

W e had bought a permit to cruise the Maddalena Islands, which are a nature reserve and reputedly beautiful, but it was late July by then, the season when half of Italy and half of France seem to descend on the islands in everything from jet skis to huge passenger ships, only a fraction of which were transmitting AIS signals.

And as for Colregs? Ha! I'm not sure they've made it as far as the Bouches de Bonifacio. We were buzzed by fast motor yachts and ancient sailing catamarans overloaded with people, so using the autopilot was never an option. Some went around us, but playing chicken with a 100m superyacht isn't my idea of fun, so we just gave way to absolutely everyone and decided not to stop.

As we headed further south along Sardinia's east coast, we gradually left the crowds behind. Our first night was spent at anchor in a beautiful bay, Cala Sabina, where we dropped the hook in 5m on sand and didn't really need to snorkel to check it as the water was so clear. We did snorkel, of course, because it was too beautiful not to, and not a jellyfish in sight.

The anchorage was busy, with maybe 20 or more yachts when we arrived, but few stayed overnight. The sandy beach was crowded in the late afternoon and evening, but we heard nothing from the beach bar, which was a relief, and the only sound as we raised the anchor early the next morning was the tiny train that puffs its way along the coast.

We stayed the next night in La Caletta, on the free pontoon just inside the entrance, so I didn't need to test my (non-existent) Italian

⚓ *Passage through Straits of Bonifacio and La Maddalena*

speaking skills. The free pontoon is a rough concrete jetty with nasty black rubber along it to act as a fender. It turned our fenders black to match and left streaks on the sides of the boat. In retrospect, we should have used a fender plank.

The next day, we battled more severe headwinds on our way to Arbatax (which I remember as 'arbour tax), where we took some time to recover from mild sunstroke and sunburn. Even a broad-brimmed hat, a long-sleeved shirt, and factor 50 fail to give enough protection when you're out in the cockpit for hours on end.

Arbatax is about halfway down Sardinia's east coast, so definitely not the closest point to Sicily, but safe stopping places aren't as frequent on this coastline as on

♠ *Chartplotter screen with a case of green measles*

the west coast, and it was August by then, so the anchorages were stuffed with holidaying Italian boats. Italian marinas are usually expensive, and we've discovered that many of them have no interest in accepting a yacht that measures less than 10m when they can charge so much more for a bigger boat. During our three-night stay in Arbatax, we were shuffled into a tighter space to make room for a more profitable boat. It's also quite hard to find potable water

here, and you need to check with the *marineros* as not all the taps provide drinking water.

As soon as we felt sufficiently rested, we set off on our longest passage yet, a distance of 178nm (around 35 hours at a cruising speed of 5 knots). As coastal sailors around Ireland and Scotland, we're used to rough seas and tricky weather, but the longest single passage we'd done up until then was less than 100nm, so this was a daunting prospect, to say the least.

At 0600, while Fraser was still sweating over the fenders, I headed *Barberry* for the exit. Just at that moment, the huge ferry that I'd assumed was going nowhere as there was no smoke from her funnels, and no sound signals, headed out across our bows, only a few boat lengths away from us. It was far too early in the morning for that sort of panic, but I swung the wheel to starboard and managed to tuck in behind her as we reached the narrow entrance. The turbulence from her prop wash caused a few *sotto voce* complaints from Fraser, but somehow we made it into the open sea and took a deep breath.

The day was perfect, with light winds (we motor-sailed to keep the speed up), but an hour into my night watch, I spotted a red glow on the horizon, and thought it must be a large ship, possibly a liner lit up for a disco – but there was nothing showing on AIS. Distances being deceptive at night,

⬥ *Co-op in Arbatax, Sardinia*

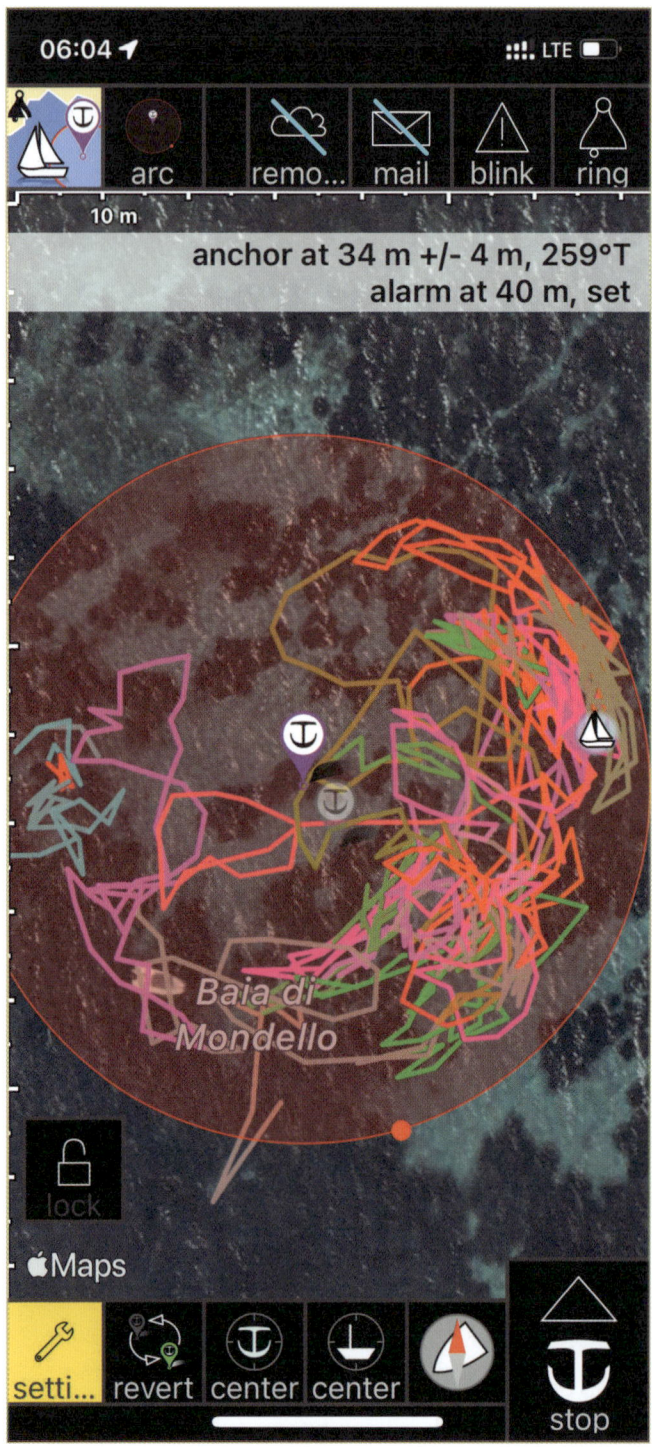

⬆ *Screenshot of our anchor app showing us in Baia di Mondello*

it seemed to be looming closer, dangerously closer, and growing in size alarmingly.

Then I realised. It was the moon, rising blood-red. My heart rate returned to normal, and I settled myself down for another three and a half hours of solitary heaven, communing with the sky. We had a calm enough crossing, at least to begin with, beneath a full moon that turned the sea to silver ripples.

The sea state worsened somewhere in the middle of the night, just as I came off watch. I'd decided to sleep in the V-berth with its comfy mattress rather than saloon berth we generally use on passage. I regretted my decision when I became airborne with every wave but was too sleepy to change positions. At least I had a soft landing on seven inches of memory foam.

We made good time and began to see the clouds that indicate land ahead by late morning. We'd failed to book a berth in a marina, so we anchored in the first supposedly sheltered bay we came to, at Capo San Vito, where we had another restless night in a heavy swell that defied the weather forecasts. Rather than stay there, and with strong winds predicted imminently, we headed another 30nm along

the coast to another supposedly sheltered bay, Baia di Mondello. There we dropped anchor in about 3–4m on a lovely big sandy patch in between areas of protected sea grass (*Barberry's* shallow draught is a huge advantage).

The forecast winds arrived early, and we spent four nights in that anchorage, gradually letting out more and more chain (only three other yachts stuck it out there with us, and they were much further out). In the end I think we had about 40m out, a scope of at least 10:1, possibly more.

The trusty old CQR didn't budge an inch as the winds climbed well into the 40 knots with gusts so strong that they flipped our dinghy over, complete with outboard. By some miracle, we were able to recover it, and nothing was lost. After a rinse with some of our precious freshwater and a good airing, followed by copious WD40, the little 2-stroke 3.5HP started up again (with only a couple of gurgling false starts) and has run faultlessly ever since. Tough as old boots.

We learned our lesson. The dinghy stays in its davits now and the outboard stays on the pushpit until it's needed.

Once the winds eased a little, we hauled in the 40+m of chain (it took a while) and set off for a marina at Cefalù. This was the only marina that replied positively to our request for a booking, and we soon discovered why. They charged us €100 for one night, and there are no facilities, no toilets or showers, and the town is the other side of the headland. If we hadn't been so desperately in need of supplies, water and fuel, we'd have stayed at anchor.

Maybe it's because we're small and scruffy, but they stuck us on the narrow end of a pontoon, at 90 degrees from all the other yachts and side-on to the swell coming into the marina. Our stern lines snatched, even though we doubled up with rubber springs to take the strain, and walking the plank to the pontoon was a challenge. At least they provided a free shuttle into the town, although it drops you a long way from any useful shops. We still had to carry our heavy rucksacks full of supplies for a hilly 1.5km to meet the shuttle for the return trip. I don't think I'd recommend Cefalù as a marina, but the anchorage would have been lovely, and the town is well worth a visit if you can cope with crowds of tourists.

We gradually worked our way along the north coast of Sicily,

→ *The Straits of Messina*

past Palermo to an anchorage at Tindari, where there are reputedly underwater statues to snorkel around. Again, the anchorage was busy when we arrived in the late evening, so we just dropped the anchor and decided it was too much hassle to swim to the statues. Too many fast RIBs that could have ploughed us down,

even if we towed a bright orange swim float.

After Tindari, which was the most sheltered anchorage we'd had in a long time, we went to a pseudo-anchorage at Calamona, almost at the far eastern tip of Sicily's north coast, and just around the corner from the Straits of Messina. This was strictly a fair-weather anchorage that provided no protection at all.

The Straits of Messina form a passage made famous in Homer's *Odyssey* for its twin monsters, Scylla and Charybdis. These two whirlpools historically swallowed ships and crews, but although the legends still cause mild panic in modest cruisers like ourselves,

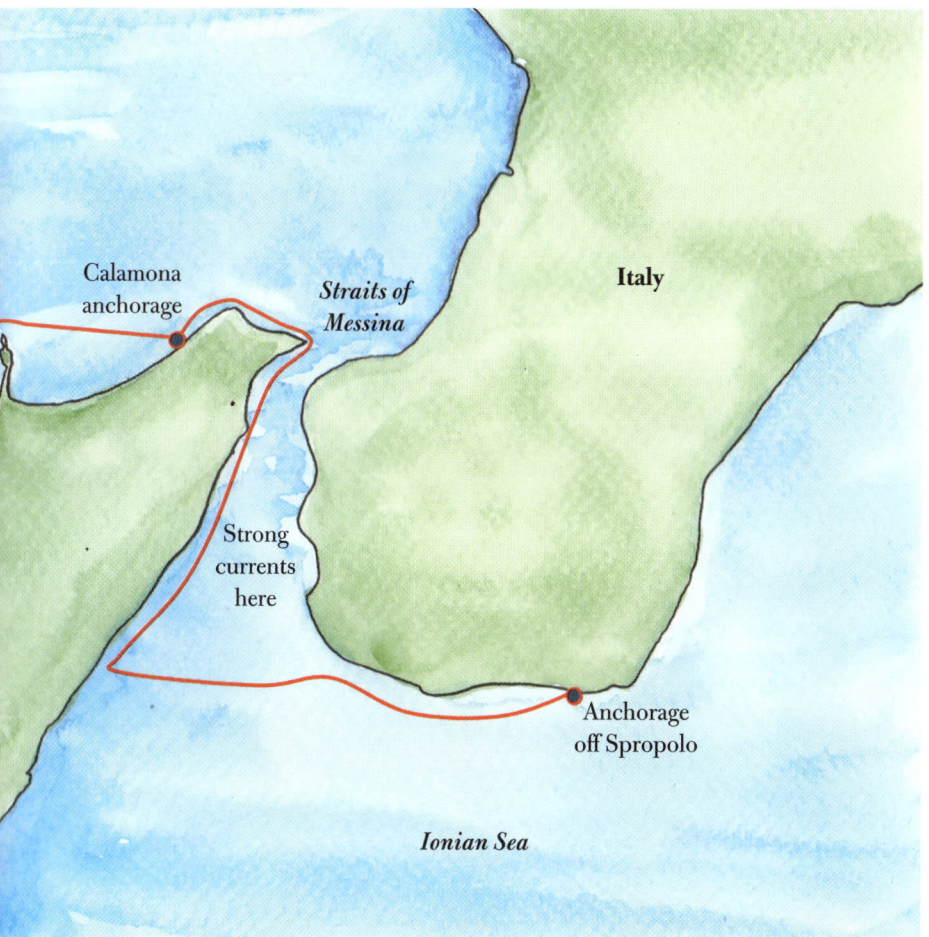

Lessons Learned

- Never assume that other boats are aware of collision regulations. Bear in mind that bit about all parties having a responsibility to take measures to avoid a collision!

- Try to avoid the busiest parts of the Med in July and August. We didn't have a lot of choice this time, but we'll not be visiting Sardinia or Sicily in peak season ever again if we can help it.

- Pick your anchorages carefully. Wind prediction models don't always take into account land features, and a bay that looks perfect on paper can often be quite exposed in reality.

- In high winds, make sure your dinghy and outboard are well secured.

- Following on from that is an observation: 2-stroke outboards are seriously hard. I mean Arnie, 'I'll be back' level of hard. They should really be wearing motorcycle leathers and reflective sunglasses.

earthquakes over the centuries have remodelled the seabed and taken much of the sting from the beasts' tails.

Here is where the Tyrrhenian and Ionian Seas meet in the narrow straits, and the difference in water levels and salinity cause a powerful surge of complex tides that can be different at different depths, hence whirlpools of fearsome reputation.

We judged our passage so we'd have the tide with us through the narrowest part of the straits but not the fastest flow, when turbulence is most noticeable. The usual anxiety about the accuracy of our tidal calculations proved unnecessary, and we flew through at 7–8 knots, whisking past swordfish hunters on the way before crossing over to Southern Italy.

Excerpts from Homer's, *The Odyssey* referring to Scylla and Charybdis

... saw a cloud of spume ahead and a raging surf, and heard the thunder of the breakers. My men were so terrified that the oars all dropped from their grasp and fell with a splash on to the sea; and the ship herself, now that the hands that had pulled the smooth blades were idle, was brought to a standstill.

* * * * *

Helmsman, your orders are these. Fix them in your mind, for the good ship's steering-oar is in your control. Give a wide berth to that foaming surf, and hug these cliffs, or before you can stop her the ship may take us over there and we'll be wrecked.

As for you, coxswain, these are your orders; attend to them, for the ship is in your hands; turn her head away from these steaming rapids and hug the rock, or she will give you the slip and be over yonder before you know where you are, and you will be the death of us.

So they did as I told them; but I said nothing about the awful monster Scylla, for I knew the men would not go on rowing if I did, but would huddle together in the hold.

* * * * *

Then we entered the Straits in great fear of mind, for on the one hand was Scylla, and on the other dread Charybdis kept sucking up the salt water. As she vomited it up, it was like the water in a cauldron when it is boiling over upon a great fire, and the spray reached the top of the rocks on either side. When she began to suck again, we could see the water all inside whirling round and round, and it made a deafening sound as it broke against the rocks. We could see the bottom of the whirlpool all black with sand and mud, and the men were at their wit's ends for fear. While we were taken up with this, and were expecting each moment to be our last, Scylla pounced down suddenly upon us and violently snatched up my six best men. I was looking at once after both ship and men, and in a moment I saw their hands and feet ever so high above me, struggling in the air as Scylla was carrying them off, and I heard them call out my name in one last despairing cry.

Samuel Butler, based on public domain edition,
revised by Timothy Power and Gregory Nagy.

A swordfish hunting boat. Note the man with harpoon at the end of a very long gantry at the front of the boat

About swordfish hunters

At first glance, swordfish hunting boats look like many of the other traditional fishing craft around these coasts, but they have two spectacular differences: They have a tall 'mast' in the centre of the boat with a crow's nest at the top, where a couple of sharp-eyed spotters scan the sea, and a horizontal gantry like a bowsprit that is often far longer than the actual boat. This is where the hunter waits with harpoon and line, ready to spear an unwary swordfish.

Between May and September, swordfish tend to hang around near the surface of the sea in mating pairs, which is what the spotters are searching for. The ridiculously long bowsprit means the hunter can get above his prey unnoticed. I'm told they target the female first as she's bigger, weighing in at around 100kg, but also because the male tends to stay close to her even after she's been harpooned, trying to protect his mate and even attacking the fishing vessel. This means the hunters can often get two for the price of one.

Swordfish hunting has been carried out in a similar manner for thousands of years, since at least the time of the Phoenicians. Although the boats have changed from the original small feluccas, with the addition of mast and gantry, the technique is much the same. Historically, swordfish hunters respected their prey and had several traditions to show this respect, but you can't help thinking that the modern-day hunters are more motivated by the price they get from restaurants for their catch than by ancient traditions. Swordfish appears on almost all menus in this part of the world and is popular with tourists.

↟ *Cefalù*

17

SOUTHERN ITALY TO GREECE

O ur next anchorage after the Straits was another pseudo-anchorage that can only be used in very settled weather as there's little protection. It had the clearest water we'd ever seen, a shade of turquoise that needs to be seen to be believed, and we fell over each other in our rush to dive into it with snorkels.

Surprisingly, after all the wonderful sea life we'd shared our dives with, there was little to see in this clear bay. One little jellyfish was the only sign of life, and luckily it was a non-stinging variety.

For the first time in a couple of months, we also noticed complete silence inside the boat. Everywhere we'd been in the Med until then, we'd heard crackling, popping sounds through the hull to some extent or other. I asked the question on a Facebook group and was told they were shrimp, feeding from the growth on *Barberry's*

hull. Pistol Shrimp, apparently, are very noisy. They have one claw much bigger than the other and they use it to stun prey with a blast of sound. They're harmless little critters, unless you're small enough to be considered a tasty morsel, but boy are they loud! The sterile clarity of this little anchorage clearly didn't support a population of shrimp.

After a peaceful night's sleep, we moved about 30nm along the coast to the first marina that seemed to have space for us since Cefalù, and it was a really lucky find. Porto delle Grazie-Marina di Roccella (Italians seem to like long names) was possibly the best marina we'd stayed in since leaving our home port of Bangor. Unusually for the Med, it offered finger pontoons, nice sturdy ones with plenty of cleats, and a pair of *marineros* come out to catch lines for you, tying up the boat so

Italy

Piccolo anchorage

Porto delle Grazie –
Marina di Roccella

Spropolo anchorage

⚓ *Italy to Greece*

Adriatic Sea

Albania

Corfu

Greece

autopilot died   Preveza Marina   *Ambrician Gulf*

Levkas

Cephalonia

Ionian Sea

↟ *Fried egg jellyfish*

you didn't even need to make the leap of faith from the side deck. The dinghy stayed in its davits, which made life much easier, and we could step ashore with no difficulty at all.

There's a small mini-market, an air-conditioned office, a café that sells drinks and ice cream, a laundry, showers, bike hire, and even a shuttle bus to the town. Beaches with golden sand stretch out in both directions, a short walk from the marina, and there are many fish restaurants nearby. We filled up with water and fuel, showered, did our washing, ate a lot of ice cream and drank a lot of beer. If we hadn't been on a mission to reach Greece, we could easily have taken out an annual contract in this marina, but after two nights of blissful sleep, we slipped our lines and headed another 50 miles east to an anchorage that gave us a good wind angle for our crossing.

Sadly, our last night in Italian waters didn't leave a great impression. We dropped anchor safely enough on sand and were happy that we were going nowhere, but no sooner had we turned off the engine than several powerful jet skis began to buzz us. Each one carried between two and four big lads out for a good time. They must have become bored of terrorising the swimmers on the sandy beach because they decided laps of the anchored yacht was a great new game.

Ignoring them, we went below to sit beneath the fans, all hatches open, and had a wee snooze. We reckoned they'd get bored more quickly if they didn't get a reaction, and sure enough they eventually went away to annoy someone else. Unfortunately, there seemed to be a party ashore that night with fireworks, followed by lots of loud music and general noisy hilarity until the wee small hours.

Yeah, I know. We're a pair of grumpy old codgers, but with advancing age we value our sleep more and more, and resent anything or anyone who gets in the way of a solid eight hours of peaceful sleep.

It was lovely and quiet when we raised the anchor at 0600 and ghosted due east into the rising sun with *Barberry's* bow pointing towards Preveza in the Ionian. This was another long crossing, 174nm, and we were not looking forward to the lack of sleep, but determined to get this last passage out of the way so we could reach our goal.

This time, we had a moonless night, which gave us a grandstand view of the myriad stars, the International Space Station as it drifted over us, and even a chain of about 20–30 bright lights that had us thinking about UFOs until we realised it was some of the many Starlink satellites that are beginning to form a network littering our night skies.

We had a following wind of about 15 knots, forecast to pick up later in the night, so we reefed both sails in readiness and used the engine to assist in keeping the speed above 6 knots. We really just wanted to reach Greece by any means at this stage, after 4.5 months of travelling through so many countries.

With a stiff wind and biggish seas, we were tossed around a bit, and Fraser struggled to sleep, having tried several different berths. Fortunately, his seasickness has not been an issue since the big swells of the Bristol Channel, but he still worries about it.

Towards the end of my watch, I became confused when my phone and wristwatch told me it was already 0130, time for Fraser to take over, but he didn't seem to be showing any signs of life. I shone a torch into the cabin, and there he was, fast asleep in the V-berth. Was he sick? Had he passed out? Then, just as he moved, shading his eyes from the torch beam and grumbling incoherently, the horrifying truth dawned on me. My watch and phone had both automatically corrected for the extra hour of time difference. It was still only 1245, not 0145. I'd disturbed my poor crew almost an hour before he was due to wake!

Fraser climbed out of bed and said he hadn't really been asleep anyway (he's a kind soul, but not always truthful). He suggested we change watches at 0100 instead of 0130, and I set my alarm an hour early to relieve him in the morning, which I did. I went out like a light despite the tossing boat and managed a fair bit of sleep before my alarm woke me.

I always wake at night with an irrational fear that Fraser has fallen overboard and is floating helplessly in his inflated lifejacket miles behind us. It's a huge relief when I look out and see him silhouetted against the stern light and know he's okay. He says he's the same with me. We wear lifejackets at night and have MOB devices attached to them that will automatically send an AIS distress signal as well as a DSC MOB call, but they've never been tested in earnest. We also clip on in bad weather or if leaving the cockpit, and also wake the other person if doing so. We should probably clip in all the time at night, but bad habits tend to creep up on one with time.

He says he has more reason to worry than me, because I've never really accepted that my disability makes me less safe clambering around the boat, and even at night I tend to take the high up route to the helm position or stand up on the aft coaming to see over the dinghy for a full 360-degree scan of the horizon. Fraser calls it monkeying around and strongly disapproves, but I really am careful to make sure I always have two solid handholds before moving my feet.

Dawn found us in sight of land. Those uncomfortable following winds had driven us faster than expected, and the mountains of Lefkada were materialising as blue shadows to the south of us (on my right). Fraser had gone below for another bit of kip, and I was enjoying the early morning, singing softly to myself. That's when I noticed the mountains to my left. They looked just like the Lefkada ones. Exactly like them, in fact.

I glanced down at the chart plotter to discover that *Barberry* had made a gentle semi-circle all by herself in the flat calm and was now heading back towards Italy. The autopilot had died without so much as a death gasp to alert me.

Hand steering now, we made landfall in Preveza Marina around lunchtime. It's hard to describe the feeling as we reversed *Barberry* into her space on the concrete dock and tossed lines to the helpful *marinero*. We were exhausted, but a quiet sense of achievement gave us a warm glow as I said *efcharistó* (thank you) to him for helping us.

Two thousand, five hundred miles, in out-of-season, cold UK tidal waters, then French rivers and canals, and finally island hopping our way across the Mediterranean

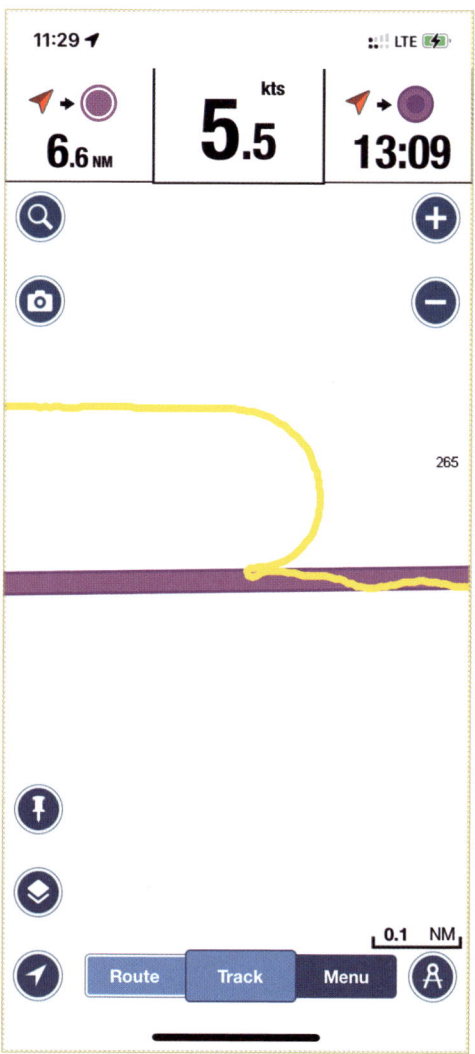

⬆ *Screenprint from chart showing 180-degree turn*

to the Ionian, where the waters are clear and the people practise the millennia-old custom of *philoxenia*, or hospitality to strangers.

We had visited 10 regions: Northern Ireland, Ireland, Wales, England, France, Corsica, Sardinia, Sicily, Italy and finally Greece and tried to make ourselves understood in four different languages (including our native English), with varying degrees of success.

After 30 years of dreaming, planning, scrimping and saving, we gradually improved our seamanship skills on a succession of boats from tiny homebuilt plywood dinghies to family-sized ketches, studied for our RYA exams, passed our CEVNI, got our ICC, and finally we'd done it.

Was there a feeling of anti-climax? Not one bit of it. We've been bitten by the cruising bug now, and the only recognised cure I know of is to slip lines and ghost away into the sunrise as often as you can manage it.

↓ *Another early start*

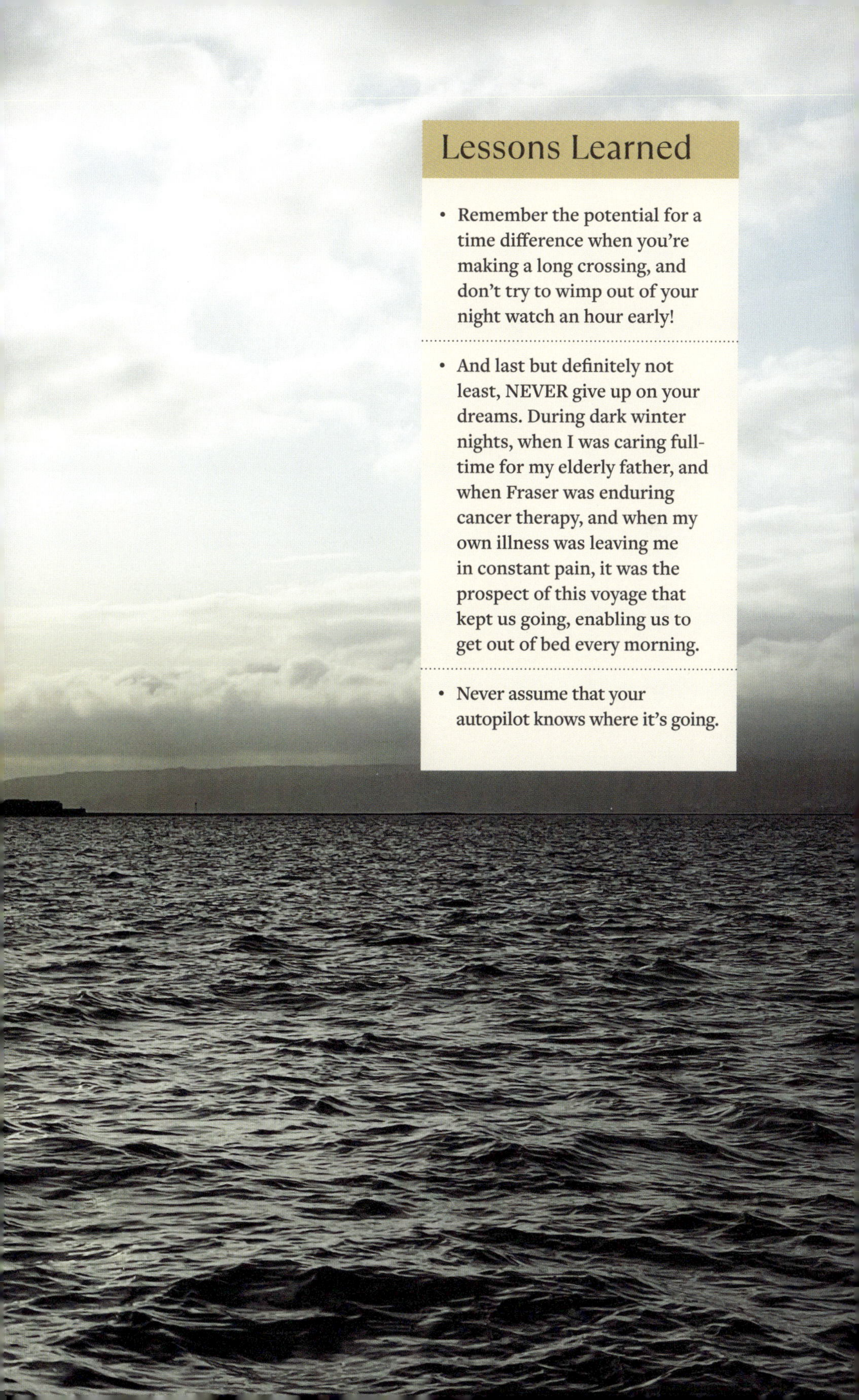

Lessons Learned

- Remember the potential for a time difference when you're making a long crossing, and don't try to wimp out of your night watch an hour early!

- And last but definitely not least, NEVER give up on your dreams. During dark winter nights, when I was caring full-time for my elderly father, and when Fraser was enduring cancer therapy, and when my own illness was leaving me in constant pain, it was the prospect of this voyage that kept us going, enabling us to get out of bed every morning.

- Never assume that your autopilot knows where it's going.

⚓ Barberry *tucked up in Cleopatra Yard, Preveza*

⚓ *Thick fog on the River Seine, leaving Honfleur*

EPILOGUE: THE DEBRIEF

Cost comparison with hiring a boat

Might it have made more sense to hire a boat if we were so keen to cruise the French canals?

Maybe it would if we hadn't already owned a suitable boat, and many people do just that every season, but we didn't *just* want to explore France, we also wanted to cruise the clear, blue, warm waters of the Mediterranean, so for us bringing our own boat through France was a no-brainer.

Prices for self-drive hire boats vary enormously, but sample quotes for smallish boats on one website (it covered quotes from several companies) came in at between £2,900 and £8,300 for two weeks in early summer 2025. This didn't include fuel and mooring costs, food, etc, so if you hired one for the six weeks we spent on the waterways, it could easily knock you back somewhere in the region of £20,000 plus, close to *Barberry's* purchase price of £21,000.

Or if the luxury of a hotel barge appeals, costs on the same website were in the region of €2,000 to €9,000 per person per week, so for two people to cruise for six weeks could rack up a bill of £20,000 to £40,000.

Were our upgrades worth it?

Looking back at the money spent to prepare for this voyage, did we regret any of the expenditure?

The biggest budget items were the new engine, the bow thruster and the new upholstery. All of these earned their keep at least as much as we'd hoped. It was a good feeling to know that the engine wouldn't let us down as we covered each of the 2,500 nautical miles through cold, turbulent seas, weed-ridden canals and finally the hot climate of the Mediterranean.

The bow thruster was truly worth every penny we spent on it. It was also worth all the flack we still get from old salts who believe it's better to get cross and hot while zig-zagging forwards and backwards, bouncing off expensive superyachts as you try to nudge into a tight space in a busy Italian marina. I'd say that if you have a long-keel yacht that's as unpredictable going astern as *Barberry*, a bow thruster could save your relationship with your crew.

The upholstery was even more of a benefit than we expected. By July and August temperatures were in the upper 30s and low 40s with no air conditioning on the boat, so we'd have probably melted like the Wicked Witch of the East from the *Wizard of Oz* if we'd still had those original vinyl seat covers. As it was, we tossed and turned in pools of sweat even with the fans going at full speed day and night.

The keel-cooled fridge was another upgrade we probably couldn't easily have managed without. In those temperatures, food would have turned in half a day without a good fridge, and we were also able to keep bottles of water in the fridge (from our UV tap) to top up our insulated drinking bottles, so we always had cool water to drink. Our water consumption probably at least tripled in the hot weather as we battled with heatstroke, and it was great to be able to trust our tank water.

We also carried an extra 50 litres of water (2 x 20-litre canisters and a 10-litre canister) lashed on deck, and these were great for cockpit showers in the evening after a sea swim. Sometimes we poured warm water from them into the solar shower bag (which would simply have been too hot if used as intended) and then took turns helping each other with the shower, or (if feeling lazy) we'd just take turns at pouring directly from the canister over each other's heads.

As *Barberry* doesn't have any form of air conditioning, we were left with electric fans as the only means to keep cool throughout the long, hot summer days and nights. Being designed for northern climes, she has only the companionway and two opening hatches for ventilation. These, of course, need fly netting at night to keep out the biting bugs. None of the side windows open and the few roof vents don't seem to contribute to airflow.

We had all hatches wide open whenever we were on the boat, but with such high temperatures we still struggled (I sweated off almost two stones in bodyweight over four and a half months). We chose a model of fans without a protective grill. They boast finger-safe blades, and they're right in so far as no one lost any fingers, but the boat was often filled with agonised yelps as one of other of us tried to squeeze past a fan in a confined space while wearing very little in the way of clothing. Best not to think too hard about that image.

Would we fit air conditioning if the budget allowed?

Possibly not. The energy consumption and space it would take up would probably put us off. Instead, we intend to sail *Barberry* in the spring and autumn, avoiding the hottest and busiest times in the Mediterranean. If someone points us towards a cheap, portable A/C unit that doesn't draw too much power, we might be tempted, but not as things stand.

The downside of open hatches is, of course, the bugs. These were especially aggressive in Port Napoléon on the south coast of France, where we spent a couple of weeks first waiting for and then re-stepping our mast. Those wee pests are vicious! We were warned that they can bite through clothing, and it's true: long sleeves and trouser legs are no protection against the Camargue mosquitoes, and they make the shark from *Jaws* look benign in comparison. Fly netting is a must.

My family generally use me as a repellent for biting insects, not because the bugs don't like me but because they like me so much that if I'm in the vicinity, they're never interested in biting anyone else. As we left the marina restaurant late one evening in June, Fraser exclaimed indignantly, 'I've been bitten!'

For once, I'd covered myself from top to toe with the strongest mosquito repellent I could buy (I used several varieties on top of each other, just to be sure), so suddenly the biting pests were prepared to settle for second best and snack on Fraser instead. I still got bitten, but I obviously wasn't quite as yummy as usual.

We bought sheets of cheap mosquito netting, cut them to size, then attached them to strips of sticky-back Velcro to cover all the hatches, including the companionway, and made sure it was all in place by late afternoon before the worst of the swarms emerged for dinner. The occasional bug still got inside, but it definitely reduced the number of bites we experienced.

With all this talk about how hot we were, you could be forgiven for asking why we fitted a diesel heater before we left on this cruise. Fraser fitted it a couple of years before we set off, so maybe it doesn't rate a mention here, but the first 4–6 weeks of our voyage were in early spring and in northern climes. It was very welcome on those chilly crossings, and it wasn't until we reached Paris in mid-May that we stopped using the heater.

What further upgrades or changes would we like to make if space and budget allowed?

A Watermaker. The UV steriliser is great, but we are still limited by the amount of water we can carry in our tanks and in canisters on deck. This was the main reason we ended up in a marina: the fear of running out of water. Having said that, we might struggle to fit one into such a small boat.

A shower fitting in the cockpit. It might seem like a luxury, but we showered in the cockpit more often than anywhere else as it was the coolest place to be. Even marina shower facilities weren't as attractive once the weather got really hot, because they were almost always the warmest places around.

Bimini. The way *Barberry's* cockpit is laid out makes a bimini a bit of a challenge, so we can't really buy a ready-made one, but need to think the design through carefully. Fraser is considering this as a winter project...

We might have said Coppercoat before we left Ireland, but as the boat will be out of the water much of the year, this seems unnecessary now. Even antifouling may be optional from now on. Every time we lift out, a good jet wash should do the trick. Better for the environment, easier on the budget and on the back. I really hate painting on antifouling! When we lifted *Barberry* out in Greece, after 4.5 months and 2,500nm, she was cleaner than we've ever seen her before. Only the propeller and the bolts for the anodes had infestations of sea creatures, and the jet wash shifted most of those too.

Electric outboard. Our trusty little 4HP 2-stroke won't last forever, especially if we continue to dunk it in the sea occasionally. When we replace it, it'll probably be with an electric outboard. Much lighter, quieter, no need to carry petrol onboard.

WiFi or Skylink setup. We still haven't worked out the best option here. Most of the setups we've researched seem quite expensive, but it would be good not to have to buy unlimited data e-SIMs for both phones. Plus, the phones don't always have good reception everywhere.

Highs and lows

Fraser

HIGHS

The feeling of travelling slowly south and getting gradually warmer. There's no comparable way to do this, except maybe cycling or walking, but then you'd be reliant on ferries.

Living in such a small space with one other person for such a long time while using so few resources. The companionship that develops should not be underestimated.

Helping Kerry fulfil her dreams kept me going even when I was seasick and miserable. Without that motivation, I'd probably have given up after the Bristol Channel.

I wanted an adventure with Kerry after decades of us both working long hours, raising a family, and in later years caring for elderly family members. Sailing seemed one of the best ways for us to have a real and memorable adventure together. It was challenging physically, mentally, and even intellectually, but we were still both able to meet those challenges despite age and disabilities. We became a surprisingly effective team.

I got excited about bread and the surprising diversity of it as we travelled through different counties.

For me, the anxiety was a downside. On longer passages, I'd worry about the weather and sea state; I'd imagine pot buoy lines getting wrapped around the propeller and stalling the engine; I'd worry about seasickness, and tiredness on night passages. OK, I'd worry about everything, but this also made me better prepared, and I left little to chance.

Being away from family for so long was a real downside, but at least we had plenty of phone calls and video calls.

Kerry

HIGHS

What I hadn't expected, although I should have, was the joy of being absorbed into so many different cultures on our way south. In France alone, the people changed, the architecture varied, and the food was a new experience at each stop. The regional variations kept everything fresh the entire way.

Island hopping from Nice to Greece brought us new perspectives. Corsica is nothing like France or Sardinia. It has elements of Italian influence, yet it's French speaking. Sardinia felt distinctly Italian, as did Sicily, but the people were very different on each island, and then different again when we reached the Italian mainland.

Night sailing was one of my highlights, but mostly in the Mediterranean. Night sailing around the UK and Ireland in April can be a cold and anxious experience, but in the Med, it's magical. Hearing a pod of dolphins breathing alongside in the darkness while water pours from their backs in streams of phosphorescent blue was simply one of the most incredible moments of my entire life. If I could have captured that feeling and bottled it, I'd have kept it to carry me through the dark winter months ahead of us, uncorking it for a sniff every so often to drive away the shadows.

Like Fraser, I missed our family. One of our daughters moved into her first house and got a new puppy, and we weren't there to help. They managed, but we really felt that we'd missed out. Our one brief visit home from Nice only served to remind us of how much we had left behind at home.

Of the pair of us, I probably had the most invested in this adventure. It had been my inspiration, my dream and I often worried that I might have dragged Fraser along in my wake. The guilt was especially powerful whenever he was seasick.

The first leg of the journey, from Bangor to Rouen, kept me on my toes. I was driving us both forwards with the anxiety of low water levels on the canals, and I hated wasting a single day waiting for the weather to improve. It didn't help that while Fraser was feeling queasy, I was still having a whale of a time.

What next?

We managed almost a whole week before withdrawal symptoms for sailing began to really itch, but this was easily solved. In years past, we'd sailed a Dockrell 17 open boat, a sweet, stable little trailer sailor that is easy to launch and retrieve, floats on a wet lawn, and sails surprisingly well. They're as rare as hen's teeth, but as luck would have it, there was one (and only one in the entire world at that time) for sale, just across the water from us in Scotland. A quick ferry ride, some negotiating, and we're now the proud owners of Clàr Innis. We're sailing again!

But we plan to fly out to Greece every spring and autumn to sail *Barberry* around the Ionian, initially, and later further afield. We'll sail the Adriatic, maybe revisit some of the places we rushed through, sail around the Peloponnese, explore the Aegean and who knows what else. It'll be good not to have a schedule driving us forward in future.

Overleaf: Getting Clàr Innis *ready to launch in Bangor, Northern Ireland*

EPILOGUE: THE DEBRIEF

APPENDIX 1

Summary of major boat costs

List of main items upgraded/added specifically for cruise

Item	Reason	Approx cost
Beta 35HP	Original Thorneycroft reluctant to start.	£9,000
Bow thruster	Long keel. Need I say more?	£4,500
Keel-cooled fridge	No fridge on boat originally, just a 1980s Coolbox with little insulation.	£880
Diesel heater	Original one damaged beyond repair.	£1,300
Solar panels Total of 200W	Old ones too small.	£450
Electric windlass	Replaced manual one.	£1,400
Holding tank	Needed for Med and for French canals.	£700
Extra freshwater tanks	200l flexible replaced with 100l flexible and 2 x 70l hard tanks.	£800
Accuva ArrowMax 2.0 UV water steriliser	Water from tanks tastes unpleasant.	£600
New upholstery and foam including memory foam bed mattresses	Old foam had flattened, and the vinyl fabric was sweaty even in Ireland.	£5,000
New dinghy and davits	Old dinghy was quite small for a fat and arthritic person (me) to feel safe in and the boat didn't have any davits.	£1,450
Safety items	Liferaft, EPIRB, MOB beacons, fire extinguishers, etc.	£2,000
TOTAL (not including cost of *Barberry*)		**£28,080**

Comments

We could have reconditioned the old engine, but the peace of mind was worth every penny.

Paid for itself when we were Med mooring, giving a degree of control astern that just isn't possible with a long-keel boat otherwise.

Not sure how we'd have survived without it. Shops were few and far between both on the French waterways and in the Med, and we'd probably have both keeled over from food poisoning without a fridge (forgive the pun).

May never use the heater again now the boat is in the Med but was a lifesaver in April in UK waters.

Without these, we would have been far more dependent on shore power for running fans and fridge. Enabled us to stay at anchor for much longer periods.

With 80m of 8mm chain, a manual windlass would have been hard work and slow in deeper anchorages. This made anchoring a pleasure.

Essential, especially in Med.

A total of 240l freshwater combined with the UV steriliser and filter gave us delicious drinking water without having to carry heavy bottled water from the shops.

Water was delicious and saved us a lot of effort. We filled water bottles from the tap and kept them in the fridge so we had plenty of cold water.

Cooler and more hard wearing, plus the memory foam bed mattress was far more comfortable to sleep on.

The davits saved us from having to choose between towing or hoisting the dinghy onto the boat and deflating it. The dinghy is the family car, and it was great to have it readily available all the time.

These are items we would have added to our inventory anyway, but we were grateful to know they were there during the long voyage and even more grateful that we didn't need to use any of them!

This only lists major items. Actual cost of upgrades was closer to £40,000

APPENDIX 1

APPENDIX 2

Costs for us

Item	Reason	Approx cost	Comments
Irish Passports	So we wouldn't be restricted by the 90 in 180-day Schengen Rule.	£530	Could have cost more but we already had several of the birth, marriage and death certificates needed.
Day Skipper theory	So we could apply for ICC.	£490	Using Navathome online.
Day Skipper Practical	As above.	£100	Mates' rates.
Yachtmaster theory	Just to see if we could.	£460	Navathome again.
ICC	To be legal in the EU.	Free	As we were RYA members at an annual cost of £55 each.
Vignette from VNF for 1 year	Toll payment for inland waterways.	£195	This covered us for the French waterways.
TOTAL		**£1,580**	

APPENDIX 3

Paperwork we carry with us

We were asked for very little until we reached Greece. Before that, we showed our Irish passports and our boat insurance documents in marinas when asked (we weren't always asked).

- Passports: Irish for entering and leaving EU countries; British for Greek bureaucracy so our papers matched the boat's registration.

- Boat registration papers (SSR in our case).

- Boat radio licence.

- Operators' radio licences.

- Boat insurance certificate translated into most European languages (our insurer, Pantaenius, provides this automatically).

- Skipper qualifications (ICC).

- CEVNI qualification if using European inland waterways.

- We also carry copies of all bills of sale relating to the boat and proof that the boat was in the EU on 31 December 2020.

We have laminated all the important documents and keep them all inside a waterproof ziplock folder inside our grab bag, along with our passports (Irish and UK).

APPENDIX 4

The Schengen shuffle

Since Brexit, the UK has become a 'Third Country' for administrative purposes, which means we no longer have limitless free movement throughout Europe. Aussies and Americans will be rolling their eyes at this stage, because this is nothing new for them.

The new state of affairs means that if you hold a UK passport only (or any non-EU passport), you are restricted to 90 days in any rolling 180-day period. This is far more difficult to keep track of than it appears on the surface, so it's safer to use a Schengen calculator to make sure you're the safe side of the rule.

This is far too complex to be covered by the scope of this book, but there are online calculators available such as this one, ec.europa.eu/assets/home/visa-calculator/calculator.htm?lang=en (be sure to read the user guide before filling in the dates).

Further information can be found on the Gov.uk website under Passports, Travel and Living Abroad and then Travel Abroad.

The application of Schengen rules has caused disruption for many UK sailors who have previously been cruising freely around the Mediterranean or through the inland waterways of Europe, hence the evolution of a new term, *The Schengen Shuffle*, by which UK cruisers spend their allotted time in the EU, then run to a non-Schengen state, eg Tunisia, Gibraltar, Montenegro, Albania or Turkey, to refresh their 90/180-day allowance.

Currently Ireland and Cyprus are the only countries with EU membership but not Schengen membership.

One way around the Schengen restriction is to apply for a long-stay visa or residency for the country in which you intend to spend most of your time. Again, it is beyond the scope of this book to cover all the options as each country has its own rules, and they can change over time.

Or you can apply for Irish passports, but for that you need to have been born on the island of Ireland, or have an Irish parent/grandparent, and it's both expensive and a drawn-out process.

APPENDIX 5

Sources of information

BOOKS, CHARTS, PILOTS AND GUIDES

The weight of all the literature we carried with us would have ballasted a small tanker. In many cases, we only needed a few pages of a pilot book, but the river and canal guides were invaluable.

It's impossible to talk about pilot guides without mentioning Tom Cunliffe (Channel) and Rod and Lu Heikell (pretty much everything Mediterranean). Rod and Lu have become good friends, and if we're stuck, a quick message almost always brings a prompt and helpful reply, often accompanied by a sketch for illustration.

Here is a list of most of the sources of information we used for our journey:

Ireland and UK
- *Irish Sea Pilot*, David Rainsbury (Imray)
- *East and North Coasts of Ireland Sailing Directions*, Norman Kean (Irish Cruising Club)
- *West Country Cruising Companion*, Mark Fishwick (Fernhurst Books Ltd)
- *The Shell Channel Pilot*, Tom Cunliffe (Imray)
- Cruising Association Forums

France
- *Through France via the Inland Waterways*, Gordon Knight (Cruising Association). Extremely useful
- Fluviacarte guides, various, although these seem to be no longer in print. There are alternatives, such as the Breil Navigation Guides
- Advice from the Women on Barges Facebook group (always excellent)
- Cruising Association Forums
- Various YouTube channels
- Michael Briant (direct communication)
- french-waterways.com is excellent for information about routes and hands-on advice

- VNF (Voies Navigables de France) website and Navi app
- Navionics on our phones or tablets and on our chart plotter

Mediterranean

- *Mediterranean France and Corsica Pilot*, Rod and Lucinda Heikell (Imray)
- *Italian Waters Pilot*, Rod and Lucinda Heikell (Imray)
- *Greek Waters Pilot*, Rod and Lucinda Heikell (Imray)
- Navily App to see up to date information on potential anchorages, to book marina berths, and to communicate with other sailors in the area

Weather

For weather, we usually used the Windy app, but caution is required as most weather apps are computer models rather than real-time observations and they can be unreliable.

Within Windy, we use the Wind Gusts layer for most sailing, but we also keep an eye on the other layers, especially CAPE Index, Thunderstorms, Weather radar, etc to spot bad weather earlier.

The Mediterranean is notorious for giving sailors either no wind at all or too much wind (and usually from the wrong direction), but this is not a problem in the inland waterways. Severe rain or drought can lead to closures of waterways, but the VNF's Navi app is a good way to find out about closures in advance.

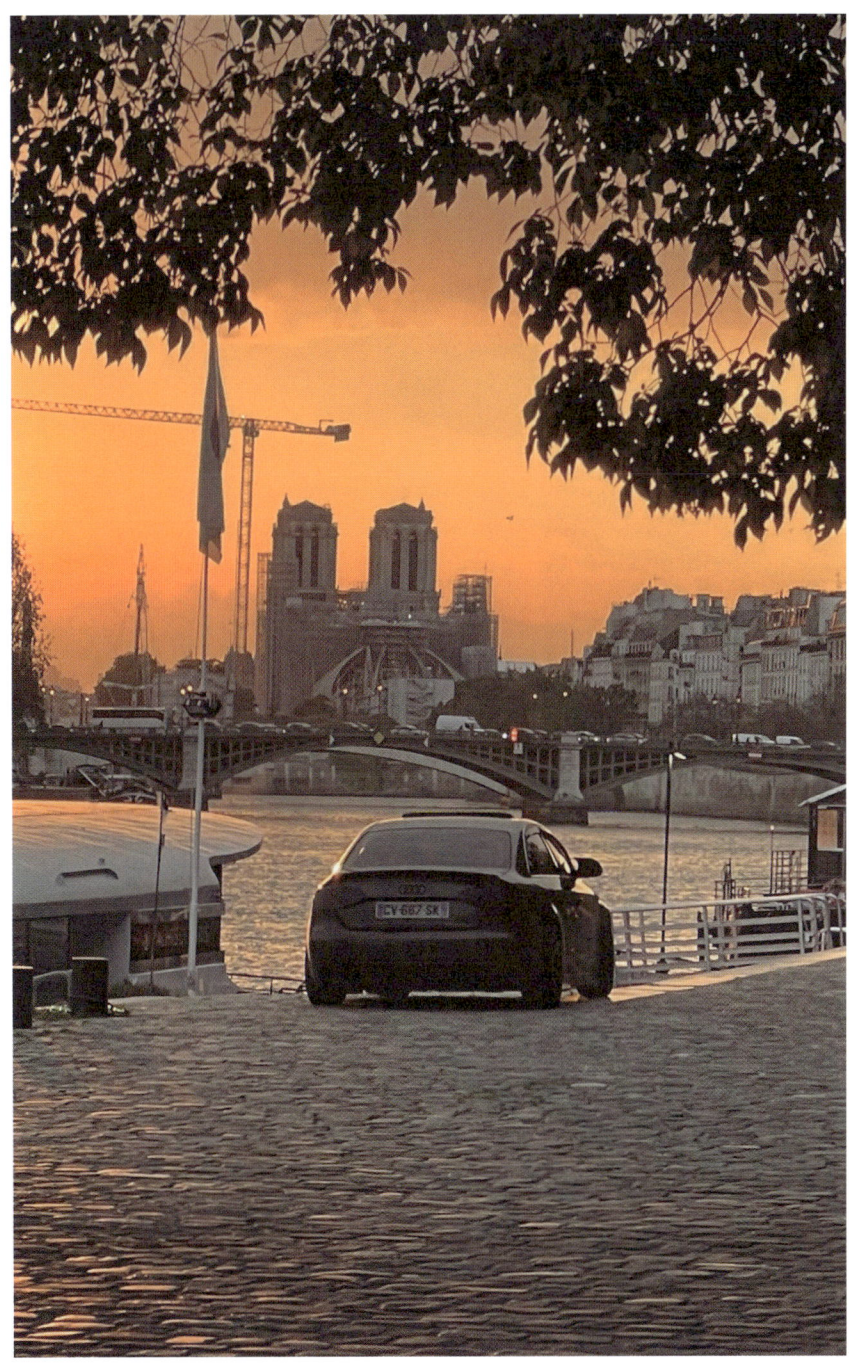

✦ *Notre-Dame Cathedral at sunset*

APPENDIX 5

ACKNOWLEDGEMENTS

Many, many people contributed to our adventures so we're almost certain to forget someone important, but there are a few stand outs without whom the whole thing would never have got off the ground.

Firstly, Rowan and Jen, who treasured *Barberry* through their 18 years of ownership and handed her over to us in the hope that we'd love her as they had. We do, but bringing her up to date and preparing her for her long voyage took more expertise than our combined skills could achieve, so the professionals stepped in to help. Brian Hanna began as a useful electronics specialist and became a friend, happily drilling holes in the hull whenever Fraser lost his nerve and chickened out. Michael Coburn, who fitted our new engine, also became a friend and, like Brian, has given freely of advice even at a distance whenever Fraser had questions.

Without Rusty McGovern's support and positive attitude, I doubt if we'd ever have gained the qualifications we needed to complete this adventure. He has so much energy and enthusiasm that we couldn't help but be dragged along with him.

The Cruising Association (CA) is a great source of information and expertise, covering everything from legal issues to tidal planning, and was especially helpful when it came to planning our route through inland France. Following on, and with some overlap, we're grateful to the members of their Women on Barges Facebook group (WOBs). The depth and breadth of their knowledge of all things inland waterways is endless. Special mention must go to Judy Evans (WOB and CA) and to Gordon Knight (CA).

Last, but by no means least, we both thank our family for putting up with our sailing obsession and for looking after our house and menagerie while we sauntered south until Fraser could jump into the sea without screaming.

INDEX

ALSO AVAILABLE FROM ADLARD COLES

Canal du Midi
By Andrea Hoffmann
9781472980038

A must-have compact travel guide to the Canal du Midi, which is recognised as one of the most beautiful and popular waterways in Europe. This up-to-date, comprehensive travel guide covers all the practical information and sightseeing opportunities boaters need to know about during their holiday on the canal.

The Adlard Coles Book of Mediterranean Cruising
By Rod Heikell and Linda Heikell
9781399404426

Rod Heikell is the undisputed expert on Mediterranean sailing and this is the complete guide for anyone cruising in the area. Thoroughly updated for its fifth edition, the book conveys the magic of Mediterranean cruising, as well as giving practical, first-hand advice on everything you need to know when sailing these enticing waters.

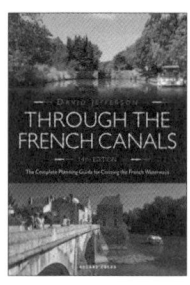

Through the French Canals
By David Jefferson
9781472981769

First published in 1970, *Through the French Canals* has been the key authoritative title on cruising the French canals ever since. This updated 14th edition is the essential comprehensive planning guide for anyone wanting to cruise through the French waterways or take their boat from the English Channel through to the Mediterranean via the inland route.

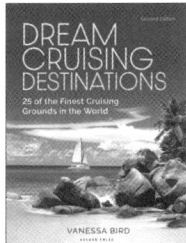

Dream Cruising Destinations
By Vanessa Bird
9781399419338

With so many wonderful destinations around the world, it is hard to know where to start, but with this book a sailor's dream can become a reality. From weekend cruises around the British Isles, and crossing the Atlantic Ocean to island hopping in the Caribbean, or sailing on one of Canada's Great Lakes, this guide gives a useful snapshot of some of the finest cruising grounds from around the world.

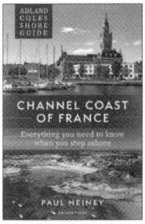

Adlard Coles Shore Guides
By Paul Heiney

Make the most of your time ashore with the Adlard Coles Shore Guides.

Channel Coast of France
9781472985699

South Brittany
9781472985736

The Netherlands
9781399409964

The West Country
9781399409995

Arriving ashore somewhere new often raises questions for even the most experienced sailor: Where are the most peaceful harbours to stop? What are the nearest shops and where can I find facilities, fuel and help with repairs? You need a different kind of pilot guide after arrival and these books are your perfect shore-side companion, helping you to explore and enjoy everything on offer.

ABOUT THE AUTHORS

KERRY BUCHANAN writes freelance for publications including *Practical Boat Owner* magazine, and her Northern Irish crime series is published by Joffe Books. She says that despite the bloodthirsty nature of her novels, she's really a very nice person, honestly. She also wouldn't have been able to produce so many novels, stories and articles if it wasn't for the support of her husband, Fraser.

FRASER BUCHANAN is a retired professor of biomaterials engineering who has always loved sailing and especially enjoys tinkering on boats. Even without a boat, he is drawn to the sea, with open water swimming being a particular passion (and a handy skill should he ever fall overboard). Although he keeps very quiet about it, he is a qualified boat surveyor and can often be spotted skulking around boatyards for fun, poking and prodding at the odd hull.